Schools, Neighborhoods, and Violence

Schools, Neighborhoods, and Violence

Crime within the Daily Routines of Youth

Caterina Gouvis Roman

LEXINGTON BOOKS

Lanham • Boulder • New York • Toronto • Oxford

LEXINGTON BOOKS

Published in the United States of America
by Lexington Books
An imprint of The Rowman & Littlefield Publishing Group, Inc.
4501 Forbes Boulevard, Suite 200, Lanham, Maryland 20706

PO Box 317
Oxford
OX2 9RU, UK

British Library Cataloguing in Publication Information Available

Library of Congress Cataloging-in-Publication Data
Roman, Caterina Gouvis, 1966–
    Schools, neighborhoods, and violence : crime within the daily routines of youth /
Caterina Gouvis Roman.
        p. cm.
    Includes bibliographical references and index.
    ISBN 0-7391-0901-4 (cloth : alk. paper)
    1. Education and crime. 2. Community and school. 3. School environment. 4.
Criminal behaior. 5. Crime—Sociological aspects. I. Title.
HV6166.R65 2004
364.9752'51—dc22

                                                                        2004013195

Printed in the United States of America

∞™ The paper used in this publication meets the minimum requirements of American
National Standard for Information Sciences—Permanence of Paper for Printed Library
Materials, ANSI/NISO Z39.48–1992.

In memory of my mother, Georgia,
who always had faith in me

Contents

Illustrations

Tables

Acknowledgments

This study would not have been completed without the continued guidance, support, and assistance of a number of colleagues and friends. I want to thank my dissertation committee—Jim Lynch and Grant Blank of American University and Bill Sabol at the United States General Accounting Office. They were always available to provide valuable comments and advice. The chair of the committee, Jim Lynch, provided endless guidance. His extensive knowledge of the criminological and sociological literature continues to amaze me. I am extremely grateful for his time and patience.

A number of individuals at the Urban Institute provided support during data collection—Gretchen Moore, Jennifer Lynn-Whaley, and Dionne Davis. In addition, Avinash Bhati spent time with me wrestling with the many methodological issues confronting this study. I owe a debt of gratitude to Blaine Liner (now retired from the Urban Institute) and Adele Harrell of the Urban Institute for providing a flexible work environment and supporting my choice to work full-time while pursuing my Ph.D.

This research could not have been possible without the data provided by and assistance of those at the Prince George's County, Maryland, Police Department. The department has a wonderful setup to assist outside researchers and a friendly staff. In particular, Carol Keeney and (retired) Corporal Larry Beverly answered my endless questions and were always willing to help with different data elements.

I have benefited greatly from a number of conversations with Luc Anselin. I cannot say enough about how generous he was in his time and advice to discuss questions I had regarding my data set in relation to spatial modeling using the software he developed, SpaceStat.

The Office of Juvenile Justice and Delinquency Prevention (OJJDP), the National Institute of Justice, and the National Science Foundation provided financial support for this study. In particular, I want to thank Barbara Allen-Hagen at OJJDP for taking an interest in this research. Most of all, this study is the product of the support and encouragement I received from my husband and coworker, John Roman. Thank you.

Chapter One

Introduction

The study of places has recently gained new prominence as a topic for study by sociologists and criminologists. Researchers are attempting to develop the appropriate theoretical and methodological tools for understanding spatial and temporal distributions of crime. Theoretical and empirical support for the importance of the social and physical environment in areas smaller than neighborhoods continues to grow. This study intends to contribute to current scholarship on the role of places in the generation of crime. This study continues the evolution of the merger of social disorganization theories and opportunity theories in explaining the crime potential of place. It refines the opportunity concepts used to determine the dangerousness of places and provides a sound framework to examine blocks as settings for crime. More specifically, this research examines the contribution of schools, operating as crime generators, to overall levels of violence within places and in the surrounding community.

Criminal opportunity theories have been used to understand the distribution of crime and violence in space. Within criminal opportunity studies, space refers to geographic units, such as the larger, more "macro" areas such as census tracts, cities, police districts, and so forth, and the smaller, "micro" area spaces that can include blocks, block faces, and particular places like intersections, buildings, and specific areas within buildings. Macro-level studies examining social disorganization provide guidance in understanding differences between high and low-crime neighborhoods. Defensible space theory, applied at the micro level or place, provides insight into the variations of crime at specific places and how specific site features (i.e., physical environment) may be linked to crime. The routine activities perspective emerged as a vehicle to understand how the confluence of circumstances surrounding the victim, offender, and place come together to create the opportunity for crime. This perspective has been applied to both macro- and micro-level places.

During the last twenty years these criminal opportunity theories have evolved to include the reciprocal relationship that exists between micro-level places and their surrounding macro-level space. Characteristics of places affect surrounding spaces, and these larger spaces affect what happens at any particular place. Certain places attract large volumes of people, generating opportunity for crime in the process. These places interact with characteristics of the environment to either inhibit crime or create even more opportunity for it.

Much of the literature that attempts to link micro- and macroplaces in explanations of crime emphasizes the social disorganization of macro-social places. The opportunity afforded by a particular microplace may be enhanced in a socially disorganized area. More recently, attention has shifted to institutions or particular types of land uses that act as attractors and generators of crime. The body of literature examining places and land uses that act as attractors and generators is steadily increasing. Studies are examining whether places like schools, bars, liquor stores, transit stations, and public housing complexes are generating crime in areas near them (Block and Block 1995, 2000; Brantingham and Brantingham 1982, 1995; Fagan and Davies 2000; Hayes and Ludlow 2000; LaGrange 1999; Roncek 2000; Roncek and Bell 1981; Roncek and Faggiani 1985; Roncek and Lobosco 1983; Roncek and Maier 1991; Roncek and Pravatiner 1989; Spelman 1995). Yet very few studies have examined how and under what circumstances these places act as attractors or generators of crime. In addition, studies utilizing opportunity theories have more often focused on property crimes rather than violent personal crimes and have excluded nonresidential areas and, instead, have focused solely on residential neighborhoods. Finally, many of these studies examine bars, liquor stores, and other commercial establishments. Relatively little attention has been given to schools. This is particularly unfortunate in that schools can tell us a lot about both crime and theories of place. Schools are present in all types of communities and are not zoned or restricted to certain neighborhoods like bars or liquor stores. Examining schools as generators of crime will allow for a greater variety of interactions between places and their social context. This study draws on criminal opportunity theories to examine how the presence of and characteristics of schools interact with the attributes of places to generate crime.

Understanding the capacity of schools to acts as generators of crime becomes even more critical with the knowledge that youth victimization may be largely related to the routines of attending school (e.g., being in school, riding on the school bus, walking to school, etc.) (Garofalo, Siegel, and Laub 1987).

If victimization of youth is highly related to the routines of attending school, then it follows that much of an area's crime may be driven by the presence of a school. All schools contain youth, and youth are crime-prone populations. Research examining how and how much schools contribute to local violence levels can serve to advance empirical criminology and provide additional mechanisms for constructing potential solutions to neighborhood violence and youth crime.

THE STUDY

This study will determine how much of an area's crime is driven by a school acting as a generator of crime. The research will address such questions as: do blocks with and near schools have characteristics that make them attractive locations for criminal behavior? Also, what is the relationship among violence, the presence of schools, other youth hangouts, and establishments nearby schools that sell goods and alcohol? Are the distances of these establishments from schools associated with victimization at specific times of the day and year? How do other features of the environment—such as the socioeconomics of an area or the nature of the schools—factor into the crime equation? For instance, do economically disadvantaged areas near schools have higher levels of victimization than less disadvantaged areas that are near schools? Are overcrowded, failing schools more likely to be generators of crime than higher performing schools? Few studies have been conducted to examine these important research questions. The need for empirical studies to explicate the contributions of place and setting is paramount to understanding the factors that influence violence.

A criminal opportunity framework is used to examine the influence of schools on block-level variations in violence. To do this, the study advances the small body of work on the integration of routine activity theory and social disorganization theory—theories that explain variations of violence across space. These theories are also "spatial" theories that adhere to the premise that crime is not random, but is clustered over space and time. These theories have not been easily integrated because the theories have been applied to understand crime clustering at different geographic levels or units of analysis—counties, cities, communities, neighborhoods, blocks, and addresses.

The human ecologists of the Chicago tradition focused on the community, and out of that tradition grew social disorganization theory, studying such factors as mobility and racial/ethnic heterogeneity (Burgess 1925; Hawley 1950; Park 1926; Schuerman and Kobrin 1986; Shaw and McKay 1942). In efforts to understand the distribution of victimization across a community, current social disorganization theorists study the dynamics among neighborhoods using measures to represent the concept of systemic control, which is essentially similar to the concept of guardianship (Bursik 1999; Bursik and Grasmick 1993; Morenoff and Sampson 1997; Sampson, Raudenbush, and Earls 1997; Sampson and Raudenbush 1999). These studies assess the dynamics that bring about systemic control but generally do so without examining the effects of physical characteristics of places. Historically, the unit of analysis was an ecological area larger than neighborhoods—the city, county, or census tract. Critics contend that neighborhoods defined as large units such as census tracts cannot capture why differences in risk of crime persist, even within a given demographic group. Social disorganization theory does not adequately address the process through which offenders and targets converge in neighborhoods (Bursik and Grasmick 1993). Findings of community differences may be erroneous in that a location or particular type of place could be causing the differences in neighborhoods.

With these limitations of social disorganization theory in mind, this study integrates other germane criminal opportunity theories in efforts to effectively address the problem of schools as generators of crime. Routine activity theory (Cohen and Felson 1979; Felson and Cohen 1980; Felson 1987; Felson 1994) emphasizes the importance of understanding the situation, which has implications for very small areas or places. According to Cohen and Felson (1979), opportunities for crime arise when three characteristics are present: a motivated offender, a suitable target, and a lack of capable guardians. The routine activity approach states that the conduct of daily activities or "routine" activities delivers the opportunities for crime to occur. Researchers have emphasized that the theory's most important contribution is that crime rates are influenced not only by the numbers of offenders and targets and the capacity for guardianship but also by the factors that affect their confluence over space and time (Sherman, Gartin, and Buerger 1989). Hence, the theory has been applied both to larger units of aggregations such as the census tract and to smaller units, such as blocks, addresses, or intersections.

There have been a number of research efforts suggesting that criminology, and more specifically—theories of crime places—can be improved by integrating the related theories of social disorganization and routine activity (Miethe, Stafford, and Long 1987; Miethe and McDowall 1993; Miethe and Meier 1990, 1994; Roundtree, Land, and Miethe 1994; Sampson and Raudenbush 1999; Sampson and Wooldredge 1987; Smith, Frazee, and Davison 2000; Taylor 1982, 1997a, 1997b, 1998, 2001; Taylor, Gottfredson, and Brower 1980; Taylor, Gottfredson, and Brower 1984). Only a few studies have used an integrated framework to examine why crime occurs in some places (or microlocations) and not others. Moreover, most of these studies of the role of place in crime generation have addressed burglary and not violence. They have also focused exclusively on the social organization and opportunity characteristics of areas and virtually neglected the role of generators. Of greater note, the studies that have examined schools and other facilities as attractors and generators of crime have generally done so with a very limited set of opportunity measures. This limits their ability to understand why and under what conditions these facilities will generate crime.

In summary, this study will advance the extant work on schools as generators of crime in places by examining how much variation in block-level crime is caused by schools, how different attributes of schools create variation in crime, and lastly, how these attributes interact with the attributes of the surrounding social and physical environment to produce crime. In addition to these issues, this the study will also advance the integration of spatial theories in a number of ways: (1) by testing theory that integrates social disorganization and routine activity theories; (2) by focusing on person-to-person violence, as opposed to property crime; (3) by expanding the focus from attributes of residential places to include crime generators; and (4) by incorporating measures representing the characteristics of schools as opposed to simply measuring the presence of schools.

In addition to advancing theory integration in a number of ways, this study also incorporates two important features to strengthen the research contribution. The study focuses on one domain of routine activities and directly incorporates a measure of time of day and year as an important dimension in variations of crime across space. Research suggests that domain-specific models will facilitate drawing the causal link between opportunity measures and victimization (Garofalo, Siegel, and Laub 1987; Gottfredson 1984; Hoyt, Ryan, and Cauce 1999; Lynch 1987) Similarly, adding a time dimension will further facilitate an understanding of the flow of offenders and targets. Extant studies on place utilize the aspect of time in a very general sense, in that temporal variables are rarely included in the models or are included to show change over a long period of time, such as years or decades.

Though this research draws on a number of criminal opportunity theories (routine activity, social disorganization, defensible space), the research is mainly a contribution to the development of theories that examine small places—whether it be blocks, block faces, or addresses. This study takes advantage of a range of detailed data, including the location of crime victimization, addresses of youth arrestees, age of arrested youth, and the characteristics of school locales. These data are used to create more precise measures of opportunity constructs. By examining both routine activity and defensible space variables, and the "structural" social disorganization variables within one domain of life activities, the research will sort out the effects of place from the structural features of neighborhood environments in terms of creating opportunity for violence.

WHAT'S TO FOLLOW

Chapter 2 reviews the theoretical and empirical research that provides a foundation for this study. Social disorganization theory and opportunities theories provide a framework for understanding variations in area crime. After discussing these theories, the chapter provides a more detailed discussion of the major constructs and measures used to operationalize neighborhood opportunity and discusses how the measures have begun to be integrated into a general opportunity theory that can address crime in small areas. Examination of the extant research assists in the selection of measures used and the development of hypotheses tested in this research.

Chapter 3 presents the research hypotheses and the data and provides a discussion of data limitations. The chapter begins by specifying the hypotheses to be tested and then discusses the research site and unit of analysis. The discussion of unit of analysis is followed by a detailed discussion of the constructs and measured used to examine how schools influence area crime. The chapter concludes with a discussion of data limitations.

Chapter 4 discusses the research methodology. First, the analytical framework is presented. The framework is used to develop the models of violent crime during different time periods of the day that correspond to the routine activities of youth. The chapter then discusses estimation techniques and the spatial models used to estimate the hypothesized relationships. Last, the chapter introduces the regression models developed to examine the research hypotheses.

Chapter 5 presents the bivariate relationships and the research findings from the instrumental variables estimation of all models. Chapter 6 provides a discussion of the findings and draws conclusions based on the study results. Overall research limitations are also discussed. The chapter closes with a discussion of the policy options supported by this study.

Chapter Two

Theoretical Foundation

HUMAN ECOLOGY AND SOCIAL DISORGANIZATION

From a historical perspective, many of the theories regarding place are based loosely on Hawley's (1950) ecological theory that views the community as a complex web of organized interrelationships that come together over time and space. Hawley's macroanalysis of human populations viewed the community as an organism in which parts all have an interrelated function. In his theory, the parts are different aspects of a community. Key aspects of Hawley's theory are the three temporal components of community structure: rhythm, tempo, and timing. Essentially, the theory states that humans and community activities have habitual patterns—rhythm, tempo, and timing—that come together to form its structure or "web of life."

Research in the mid-1900s examining crime and the environment or "social organization" developed ecological models to explain their findings that delinquency was related to areas (or places) that were witnessing decay and physical deterioration. The decaying areas were closer to the central city (Shaw and McKay 1942). White (1932), examining offender rates, found that opportunity for crime was related to community structure and a community's location within a larger community. These and other studies (Burgess 1925; Thrasher 1927; Lander 1954; Bordua 1958; Schmid 1960; and Chilton 1964) provided the basis for understanding how crime is related to the environment—physical or social. Shaw and McKay did not expressly include the ecological dynamics that distribute criminal opportunities across space in their model of social disorganization (Bursik and Grasmick 1993), but their ecological research helped further the discussion that certain places have features that come together to create opportunity for crime.

Contemporary proponents of social disorganization theory (Bursik and Grasmick 1993; Morenoff and Sampson 1997; Sampson, Raudenbush, and Earls 1997; Sampson and Raudenbush 1999) draw on Albert Hunter's (1985) three-level approach to local community social control that includes three levels or aspects of control: the "private" level, the "parochial" level, and the "public" level. These levels, or processes, help illuminate the somewhat complex layering of different community dimensions, all of which have an impact on social ties and the development of informal social control across neighborhoods. The private level represents the social support and mutual esteem derived from interpersonal relationships among residents; the parochial level represents the role of the broad interpersonal networks that are created through the interlocking of local institutions, such as stores, schools, churches, and voluntary organizations; and the public level focuses on external resources and the ability of a neighborhood to influence community and government agencies in their allocation of resources to neighborhoods. The interplay of these three levels is a dynamic process that is differentially realized across neighborhoods (Sampson and Raudenbush 1999). The willingness of residents to act together or cohesively for the common good of the neighborhood becomes a key feature of social disorganization theory termed "collective efficacy." Collective efficacy links neighborhood cohesion and mutual trust with the developed beliefs and common expectations among residents for intervening to support informal social control (Sampson and Raudenbush 1999, 612–13). Neighborhood structural processes (e.g., residential stability, economic advantage) and collective efficacy act together to form a type of guardianship similar to the guardianship construct in routine activity theory (Cohen and Felson 1979; Felson 1987; Brantingham and Brantingham 1995).

OPPORTUNITY THEORIES

Much of the theoretical support for the predictability of criminal events comes from criminal opportunity theories that have been modeled to account for individuals' risks and aggregate rates of predatory crime. Opportunity theories can be very generally categorized as theories that aim to explain variations in crime as due to: (1) site features, (2) victim lifestyles or routine activity, and (3) the predisposed structural dynamics of proximity and exposure as related to offender choice.

Site Features

Research has demonstrated that certain site features are associated with higher crime rates, or are more vulnerable to crime, either because they contain spaces conducive to criminal activity or spaces that are not defensible against predators (Greenberg and Rohe 1984; Greenberg, Rohe, and Williams 1982; Mawby 1977; Taylor, Gottfredson, and Brower 1984). The physical environment includes internal and external features and layouts of buildings, boundary characteristics, and traffic patterns. The body of research relating to the location of targets and movement of offenders and victims in space and time includes research on event-based preventive approaches to crime, such as "defensible space" (Newman 1972), "crime prevention through environmental design" (Jeffrey 1971), and "situational prevention" (Brantingham and Brantingham 1991; Clarke 1980, 1992; Mayhew et al. 1976). These approaches or theories began to take shape as findings emerged showing the importance of focusing research on high-crime areas. Research on census tracts in St. Louis that focused on those neighborhoods where most crimes were committed (Boggs 1965) found that offenders consider their targets in terms of familiarity and the potential for profit. Within the next decade two books emerged that addressed the importance of understanding criminal targets and the opportunities created by certain places. Oscar Newman's Defensible Space (1972) and Thomas Repetto's Residential Crime (1974) discussed the relationship of physical design to successful criminal victimization.

Defensible space theory posits that physical features such as certain types of design, layout, and circulation patterns can make people more vulnerable to victimization (Newman 1972; Jacobs 1961; Perkins, Meeks, and Taylor 1992). Features that offer better capability for surveillance, demarcation between public and private space, open spaces divided into easily controlled space, proximity of space or structures to other well-used locations, and areas that are less permeable are less likely to provide the opportunity for victimization (Taylor, Gottfredson, and Brower 1980; Taylor and Gottfredson 1987; Newman and Franck 1982). Cross-sectional and longitudinal studies examining internal layouts, boundary characteristics, and traffic patterns of neighborhoods found that the internal layouts of low-crime areas provided less access to foot and car traffic—more one-way, narrower, and lower volume streets—than those found in higher-crime neighborhoods (Greenberg and Rohe 1986; Greenberg, Williams, and Rohe 1982; White 1990). Molumby (1976), examining a large college apartment complex, found that apartments and townhouses located on blocks with numerous entrance and exit points were victimized at a much higher rate than those with fewer access points. Newman's work also emphasized that symbolic barriers can prevent a place from becoming a target.

Defensible space theory forms the basis for research examining how different land uses (e.g., commercial, residential, mixed), as well as density of the physical environment (e.g., housing density), influence crime.

Victim Lifestyles and Routine Activities

The second category of opportunity theories includes lifestyle theory, put forth by Hindelang, Gottredson, and Garofalo (1978), and routine activity theory (Cohen and Felson 1979). Lifestyle theory focuses specifically on varying lifestyles of different social groups and how the different lifestyles are related to the differential exposure to dangerous places, times and other individuals. Lifestyle is "routine daily activities, both vocational activities (work, school, keeping house, etc.) and leisure activities" (Hindelang, Gottfredson, and Garofalo 1978, 241). Antecedents of lifestyle are important because they include the behavioral expectations of people occupying differing social roles, the behavioral constraints imposed by class or social status, and how individuals adapt to the behavioral and structural constraints (Maxfield 1987a, 1987b). Other researchers, including Garofalo, later discussed the importance of perceptions about crime and behavioral reactions or adaptive behavior by individuals in different circumstances (Balkin 1979; Cook 1985; Garofalo 1987).

Very similar to lifestyle theory is routine activity theory, which focuses on the context where potential victims and offenders come together in the absence of guardians. Routine activity focuses on the conduct of daily activities or "routine" activities not only for the victim, but for the offender and guardian, as well. In other words, the presence (or absence) of motivated offenders, potential targets, and guardians depends on the activities in which people are engaged and other characteristics of an area. Cohen and Felson define routine activities as "any recurrent and prevalent activities which provide for basic population and individual needs, whatever their biological or cultural origins" (1979, 593). To understand the contexts where crime occurs, studies often include measures of proximity — proximity to motivated offenders or proximity to potential victims.

The aspect of guardianship is crucial to understanding the routine activity framework (Felson 1986, 1987). Guardians can be classified as intimate handlers, guardians, or place managers. Intimate handlers have direct and personal influence over offenders. Offenders will be less likely to commit crimes in the presence of intimate handlers such as teachers, employers, or parents. Guardians are people who act in the formal sense as guardians — such as police or private security guards. But guardians can also be friends or peers who act as guardians for protection of each other, for example, a friend walking another friend home. Place managers manage places, such as doormen, apartment managers, or janitors and lifeguards. For crimes to occur, whether the crimes are property or violent crimes, guardians have to be absent, ineffective or negligent (Eck 1994).

Structural-Choice

Theories integrating a focus on victim, offender and situation include the work of Miethe and Meier (1990, 1994) to develop a structural-choice model of victimization. Their model is very similar to lifestyle and routine activity models with the minor exception that the structural choice model views proximity and exposure as "structural" features that predispose individuals to riskier situations, and views attractiveness and guardianship as "choice" components that determine the selection of a particular crime target within a sociospatial context. They argue that it is important to include both measures of individuals' lifestyles and contextual variables in studies of victimization.

Miethe and Meier were not the first to discuss or examine contextual variables when studying victimization. Sampson and Wooldredge (1987) analyzed data from the British Crime Survey, which provided the opportunity to examine community-level variables without relying on census measures. They found that personal burglary risk was higher for those individuals living in areas with high family disruption, single family households, and high density of VCRs. Smith and Jarjoura (1989), also examining personal burglary risk found a number of neighborhood factors to be important. Simcha-Fagan and Schwartz (1986), though not integrating routine activity variables, examined the effects of community structural characteristics (i.e., social disorganization measures) on aggregate and individual delinquency. These studies examining contextual variables are important because they set the stage for integration of theories of crime—particularly social disorganization theory and routine activity theory. These theories have the same overarching goal: to explicate the relationship between neighborhood and individual characteristics and levels of crime in light of opportunities provided by the environment.

OPPORTUNITY CONSTRUCTS AND THE EVOLUTION OF THEORY INTEGRATION

Over the years, the works of lifestyle theorists, routine activity theorists, and structural choice theorists have become more closely aligned so that the major concepts and constructs underlying their studies are generally one and the same. Because the constructs in social disorganization theory are contextual influences that increase the risk of crime, these constructs—such as unsupervised peer groups, economic deprivation, and single-parent families—have also fallen under the rubric of opportunity. The following sections provide a summary of the constructs and measures used to operationalize opportunity models and a brief discussion of limitations.

The Constructs

Proximity to crime

Opportunity theories posit that victimization increases with the physical proximity to high-crime areas. High-crime areas have generally been defined as areas with a large population of potential offenders. Social disorganization theory suggests that high-crime areas are characterized by high levels of residential instability or population turnover, ethnic heterogeneity, and low socioeconomic status. Hence, measures of proximity in the social disorganization literature generally have been demographic in nature. For instance, areas with a large number of young people have been used in some studies as a proxy measure for proximity to offenders because research has shown that young people or teenagers are more likely to commit crimes.

Routine activity suggests that even within large geographical areas such as neighborhoods, there can be great variation in levels or rates of crime. Places can foster a decrease in social control or act as magnets for unsupervised groups of people who can become "motivated offenders" (Cohen and Felson 1979). These institutions include, for instance, schools, bars and liquor stores and even quasi institutions such as public housing and other subsidized housing projects. Thus, proximity to these places can influence the amount of crime (Felson 1987, 1994).

In addition to social disorganization studies, routine activity studies examining proximity as an opportunity construct also have used measures such as place of residence and socioeconomic characteristics such as the unemployment rate or racial composition, and measures of perceived safety of a neighborhood (see Cohen, Kluegel, and Land 1981; Hough 1987; Lynch 1987; Sampson and Wooldredge 1987; Miethe and Meier 1990). Miethe and Meier (1994, 47) state that the best single indictor of proximity is the average rate of offending in an individual's immediate neighborhood but that self-report or official measures are rarely available at the neighborhood level. A representative measure for the motivated offender construct has not been developed in the routine activity literature. Data collection procedures for national studies on victimization in the United States have not been designed to

capture neighborhood or block variation (see discussion in Bursik and Grasmick 1993, 73–77). Use of official records on arrestees requires confidential
data and resource intensive address cleaning. Groff and LaVigne (2001) used
coded addresses of burglary arrestees for their examination of the spatial patterns of burglary in a small neighborhood. For areas with a high number of
burglaries, more than three-fourths of the burglarized addresses were close to
likely offenders. However, their measure was limited in that the burglary arrestee data had very little variability across their unit of analysis (grid cells).

Exposure to crime

Exposure to crime represents the visibility and accessibility to crime which
has implications for the amount of time spent in a certain place (Cohen and
Cantor 1980, 1981; Cohen, Kluegel, and Land 1981; Hindelang et al. 1978;
Kennedy and Forde 1990; Miethe et al. 1987) and the physical characteristics
of a place that make a potential victim be more exposed to a potential offender (Brantingham and Brantingham 1991, 1994, 1995; Sherman, et al.
1989). Many studies examining exposure to crime have used measures of an
individual's primary daily activity—what Hindelang and colleagues have
called "lifestyle." These studies posit that individuals who go to work or to
school—and hence, spend more time away from home—have greater exposure to crime. An increase in exposure, everything else held constant, leads to
an increase in victimization. Miethe, Hughes, and McDowall (1991) examining aggregate rates of crime, conducted a study using city-level data and operationalized exposure using three separate measures that included: (a) the
percent of civilian labor force that is female, (b) the percent of employees
who use public transportation, and (c) the average sales from eating and
drinking establishments per resident. They found that the net impact of exposure varied across the different indicators and crime types. Higher rates of female labor force participation were associated with decreases in crime rates.
Higher sales from food establishments was the only variable significantly associated with higher burglary rates, and high rates of public transportation
were related only to increased rates of homicide and robbery. Other studies
examining aggregate crime rates have operationalized exposure as the supply
of entertainment establishments and youth-related places (LaGrange 1999;
Messner and Blau 1987; Smith, Frazee, and Davison 2000). However, these
studies only included measures for the numbers of places, not measures of
distance (from unit of analysis, e.g., tract, block, neighborhood) to the nearest place(s) of interest.

Miethe, Stafford, and Long (1987), using data from the National Crime
Survey, found an interaction between demographic characteristics of victims
and exposure in terms of nighttime activities away from the home, but only

for victims of property crime, not predatory crime. In contrast, Kennedy and Forde (1990), using more detailed data from the Canadian Urban Victimization Survey, found that routine activity variables of nighttime activities were significantly related to predatory crime (robbery and assault). However, neither study examined the time of day when the crime occurred, but simply examined the aggregate relationship between number of hours out at night and criminal victimization.

In addition to lifestyle-type variables, measures for exposure have also included measures of physical characteristics that enhance or impede visibility or accessibility (Greenberg, Rohe, and Williams 1982; Hough 1987; Repetto 1974; Taylor and Hale 1986; Taylor, Schumaker, and Gottfredson 1985; Waller and Okihiro 1978). Physical characteristics related to exposure include types of land uses and housing characteristics that provide more accessibility for potential offenders. Exposure has also been measured through the use of physical objects, such as locks, fences, alarms, guard dogs, effective street lighting, or anything else that acts as target-hardening agents.

Capable guardianship

Within opportunity theories, capable guardianship represents the ability of persons to prevent crime from occurring. Guardianship generally refers to person characteristics of the household, place, or neighborhood where people act in the capacity of guardians. The presence of collective activities, such as block watches, is also a form of guardianship. Many studies utilize household size variables to measure guardianship. As the number of individuals within a household increases, the number of capable guardians increases (Miethe, Hughes, and McDowall 1991; Miethe and Meier 1990). Some studies examining routine activity variables have used marital status as a proxy for guardianship in the sense that being married means there is additional capacity for guardianship (Miethe, Stafford, and Long 1987).

Studies examining guardianship show inconsistent results (Cohen, Kluegel, and Land 1981; Greenberg, Rohe, and Williams 1982; Miethe, Hughes, and McDowall 1991; Popkin et al. 1995; Reppetto 1974; Sampson and Wooldredge 1987; Sampson 1985, 1986; Sampson and Raudenbush 1999; Skogan and Maxfield 1981; Taylor and Hale 1986; Taylor, Schumaker, and Gottfredson 1985). Miethe, Hughes, and McDowall (1991) found that household size was a strong predictor of the level and changes in official rates of homicide, robbery, and burglary. Popkin and colleagues (1995) evaluated crime prevention efforts in several crime-ridden public housing complexes and found that guarded stations and tenant patrols helped reduce violence. Studies evaluating the use of guards and security attendants in parking lots have found reductions in car-related crimes (Barclay et al. 1996; Laycock and Austin 1992; Poyner

1991, 1994), but none of these studies examined personal violence. Efforts to reduce repeat burglaries by stepped-up patrolling has also showed some evidence of success (Anderson, Chenery, and Pease 1995b).

Target attractiveness

Last, opportunities theories model a target's attractiveness. Target attractiveness is the material or symbolic desirability of persons or property targets to motivated offenders. Attractiveness also includes the physical properties of a target that make it easily portable. Target attractiveness is often a central component for opportunity studies examining property crimes, such as burglary or larceny, but less so for interpersonal crimes like assault. Attractiveness with regard to individual victims has been proven to be a difficult construct to conceptualize (cf. Kennedy and Forde 1990). For this reason, a more detailed literature review is not provided.

Theory Integration and Explication

Studies probing the aspects of guardianship, exposure, and proximity have been criticized on the grounds that the central components have overlapping aspects and confounding relationships. For instance, something that is well-guarded has less exposure. People within proximity to potential offenders are more exposed. People in high-density housing may be more exposed to motivated offenders, but there are, at the same time, more potential guardians. Hence, it has been difficult for studies built on an opportunity framework to adequately measure the central variables (Bursik and Grasmick 1993; Massey, Krohn, and Bonati 1989; Maxfield 1987b).

Similarly, the social disorganization construct of collective efficacy is closely aligned with the guardianship construct in routine activity. At the street block level, nonresidential land use or increased housing density may impede residents' ability to be distinguish between strangers and those who belong in the neighborhood (Greenberg, Rohe, and Williams 1982; Taylor, Schumaker, and Gottfredson 1985; Taylor and Hale 1986). Reduced ability to recognize other neighbors has been associated with neighborhoods with less social control and more crime (Kurtz, Koons, and Taylor 1998; Roncek and Bell 1981; Roncek and Faggiani 1985; Taylor 1988). Crowded neighborhoods and decreasing social control are important concepts for social disorganization theory because crowded neighborhoods and neighborhoods with high residential turnover have less ability for residents to bond collectively and increase the potential for community-based informal social control. Reduced collective efficacy plays out as less human guardianship against criminal elements, whether it is unsupervised youths hanging out on corners or strangers coming to the door. In other words, neighborhoods low in collective efficacy have less ability to deter crime. Areas of low collective efficacy and higher crime have been characterized as very urban or close to a central city, racially heterogeneous, having high residential turnover, and with a larger percentage of female-headed households (Sampson and Raudenbush 1999; Morenoff, Sampson, and Raudenbush 2001; Sampson, Raudenbush, and Earls 1997).

Today, research is attempting to use better data in order to create stronger operationalizations of both social disorganization variables and routine activity variables to avoid confounding relationships (Sampson 1985, 1986; Sampson and Raudenbush 1999; Smith, Frazee, and Davison 2000). The ability for studies to distinguish types of human guardianship (i.e., handlers, guardians, or place managers) can aid in which processes are related to crime reduction (Eck 1994). Smith et al. (2000) distinguish between person density per household and structural density by using detailed tax assessment data on land parcels combined with census indicators. Address and parcel-based data can be aggregated up to any level of study and generally provide sufficient variation for multilevel studies.

This study attempts to overcome some of the limitations previous research has encountered in specifying appropriate opportunity constructs. Care was taken in operationalizing the critical routine activity construct of motivated offenders and reduced capacity for guardianship, as well as in defining other physical environment variables that may increase the opportunity for offending. The extant research includes only a limited number of studies that utilize the wealth of available address-level data to examine violent crime at units of analysis smaller than block groups. Chapter 3 details the measures used to specify the critical opportunity constructs.

Research on crime opportunity can also be advanced by theoretical integration. A growing body of literature is attempting to integrate social disorganization and routine activity theory by examining interaction effects (LaGrange 1999; Smith, Frazee, and Davison 2000; Miethe and Meier 1994; and Miethe and McDowall 1993). These studies emphasize the importance of continuing research that examines individuals' activities (i.e., routine activities) with regard to neighborhood context. The studies suggest that research can examine the interaction between individual-level and neighborhood-level factors as multilevel studies or, examine interactions between routine activity variables and social context (social disorganization) variables in aggregate data studies. By utilizing interactions, one can specify that relationships hypothesized under one theory are conditional on values derived from a variable from a different theory. It is not improbable to believe that relationships found among land use variables would be contingent on neighborhood structural constraints (e.g., social status of a neighborhood). Crime may be strongly associated with the presence of liquor stores, for instance, but in affluent neighborhoods, the relationship may disappear. Similarly, social disorganization theory may link racial heterogeneity to socially disorganized areas high in crime, but with regard to youth activities and crime, the relationship my exhibit different tendencies in areas where there are large numbers of youth. Youth congregating at school bus stops in racially heterogeneous areas may be at great risk of violence, given the possible tensions between youth of difference races.

Miethe and McDowall (1993) found that the effects of security measures and living alone are reduced in land uses that are a mix of residential and commercial. In a block-level model examining how routine activity theory and social disorganization variables influence robbery, Smith, Frazee and Davison (2000) found five out of twelve interaction terms tested to be significant. The authors hypothesized that the number of single-parent households and distance from the center of the city would interact with land use variables that included the number of motels; the number of stores; the number of vacant/parking lots; the number of multifamily residential housing; the number of bars, gas stations, and restaurants; and the number of commercial places. They found that increases in distance from the center of the city reduces the crime generator properties of multifamily housing, bars, gas stations, and vacant/parking lots.

In summary, integration of social disorganization and routine activity theory can provide clarity in explicating the dynamic processes of places. Examination of interaction effects provides useful information on situational contexts that can be useful in suggesting causal relationships. Motivated offenders may only operate in very specific situations, depending on a large number of factors that have to converge. Similarly, individual activities may not predict risk in certain areas because sufficient opportunity already exists to increase the risk of victimization.

OPPORTUNITY AND VIOLENT VICTIMIZATION

Although a large number of studies use opportunity frameworks to examine burglary, routine activity approach first was applied to direct contact (person-to-person) predatory offenses, which requires at least one person to wrongly take or damage the person or property of another. Felson rearticulated that the approach also applies to violent crimes (Felson 1987). Fights or assaultive behavior are more likely to occur without the presence of peacemakers or in the absence of intimate handlers.

Messner and Tardiff (1985), in their examination of detailed records of homicides, found support for the routine activity approach. A few years later, Messner and Blau (1987) found that increased activity outside the household was related to increased rates of homicide, rape, robbery, and aggravated assault. As described earlier, Kennedy and Forde (1990) found that participating in certain nighttime activities increased the risk of robbery and assault. Smith, Frazee, and Davison (2000) found that street robbery was the result of a combination of both social disorganization and routine activity factors. Some theorists, however, have questioned the appropriateness of opportunity theories for examining interpersonal violence (Birkbeck and LaFree 1993; Miethe and Meier 1994) and have criticized past studies finding links between opportunity constructs and violence for using poorly developed measures and hence rendering the results difficult to interpret. These criticisms provide a strong case for additional studies using more rigorous data elements necessary for the advancement of the routine activities approach.

THE REEMERGENCE OF THE ROLE OF PLACE

Fortunately, new resources are becoming available that facilitate the development of more precise indicators of opportunity. As a result, studies examining blocks as microenvironments of crime are growing in number. Data collection efforts and the level of analyses of geographic data are becoming more sophisticated. Large mainframe computers are becoming standard in police agencies and computer mapping of criminal events is rapidly expanding as a tool for crime analysis for both police practitioners and researchers. Geographical information system programs are advancing alongside of increased availability of up-to-date, digitized street maps. Simultaneously, hardware and software prices are decreasing. With these advances, hundreds of thousands of crime incidents can be analyzed at specific locations. In addition, the characteristics of specific locations can be analyzed because the current data and systems environment provide the opportunity to link multiple data sources, regardless of data type.

The groundwork for understanding crime at specific locations or small places had been laid years earlier. Ecological psychologists had been trying to understand how places function since the late 1940s (Barker 1968; Barker et al. 1943; Wicker 1979, 1987; cf. Taylor 1998). They were examining "behavior settings," or natural units of the environment that exhibit recurring patterns of behaviors within the surrounding physical environment. Also, in the late 1970s and early 1980s a series of studies were published examining the "defensibility" of defensible space, and from those studies a theory of human territorial functioning was developed (Taylor 1980, 1983, 1988) that merged ecological psychology with criminology. In many ways, the early work on defensible space (Newman 1972) was being reexamined in light of the recently developed opportunity frameworks of lifestyle and routine activity. Territorial functioning examined the social and physical processes of neighborhood blocks. Variability in block-level processes was substantial. Elements of self-protection and defense were found to be block-level processes. Variation in different processes across blocks resulted in different outcomes, whether the outcome examined was crime and disorder or neighboring and social ties. Other researchers were or had been coming to the same conclusion, and microlocations such as blocks, and block faces, and even single addresses, became the focus of research for understanding opportunity structures (Brantingham et al. 1976; Gottfredson 1981; Roncek 1981; Roncek and Maier 1991; Sherman, Gartin, and Buerger 1989).

As block-level research advanced with Taylor's work, researchers became aware that to understand the ability of blocks to defend themselves, it is important to understand the larger environmental context. The importance of theory integration was amplified. Focus returned to research on facilities that demonstrated relationships between types of crime and community institutions such as schools, bars and taverns and public housing complexes. With regard to schools, studies found that residential areas that were adjacent to public high schools had higher crime rates than areas that were more than one city block away from these schools (Roncek and LoBosco 1983; Roncek and Faggiani 1985). The studies used dichotomized measures of adjacency (i.e., primary adjacency versus non-adjacent; secondary adjacency versus nonadjacent) to examine the effect of schools on crime. The studies controlled for a number of social composition variables (value of owner housing, race, single-person households, number of elderly) and residential environment variables (density, overcrowding, extent of apartment buildings, vacancy rate, number of nonresidential land uses). Enrollment size was the only school characteristic incorporated into the authors' models. Roncek and colleagues found that enrollment size did not have a significant effect on the amount of crime in neighboring blocks. In a more recent study examining block proximity to schools in Brooklyn, Roncek (2000) found that all types of schools (public elementary, junior and senior high schools, and private grammar schools), except private high schools, had significant effects on levels of crime.

A detailed study examining land parcels in Carlsbad, California, found that parcels occupied by middle and high schools were crime generators (Weeks et al. 2000). Residential parcels in close proximity to school parcels experienced an increase in assaults and burglaries. In studies examining other crime generators, Roncek and Bell (1981), Roncek and Pravatiner (1989), and Roncek and Maier (1991) found that the number of recreational liquor establishments on residential city blocks had a positive effect on the amount of crime. The authors also found that when they examined only blocks with bars, the concentration of apartment buildings and size of the block had a large effect on the distribution of violent crimes across blocks. The authors concluded that decreased guardianship and high levels of anonymity were important factors to consider when examining crime.

Similarly, a study of public housing projects (Roncek, Bell, and Francik 1981) found that proximity to public housing had a small, but significant, effect on the distribution of violent crime and that the number of housing units also influenced the distribution of violent crime. Social and structural variables characterizing the housing projects were weak predictors of violent crime rates. The authors suggested that more research needs to be done to examine the interactions between the structural characteristics of the areas and the projects themselves and the dynamic social exchanges that occur in different ecological settings.

Routine activity theory provides the framework to understand how these community institutions can be attractors and generators of crime. There are periods of the day or week, and so on, where offenders can easily avoid their handlers. Hence, certain routine activities, by definition, evade informal control. This is the case for youth walking to school, congregating at a bus stop, or hanging out in the evening with peers, out of the range of parental supervision (Felson and Gott-fredson 1984). Felson describes how the urban environment has evolved over the decades, into what he calls the Great Metropolitan Reef. "Young delinquents flow rather freely about the metroreef, drawing illegal sustenance readily from its rich stores and routine activities" (1987, 917).

As the reef proliferates:

> it moves offenders, targets, guardians and handlers about so quickly that it creates tremendous imbalances in crime risk. Some spots are very risky, letting offenders find ready targets. Worse still, some spots appear to draw or assemble offenders and targets, while dumping the resulting offenses on the neighbors....If schools are great producers of property crime, official . . . data indicate that very little ends up assigned to the schools themselves. It appears that certain organizations suffer a fraction of the crime they probably "help" to produce, are assigned little statistical credit for their "contribution" to crime production. (1987, 920–21)

Research has linked large and impersonal school settings with violence (Alexander and Curtis 1995; Olweus 1993; Newmann 1981). A recent study examining violence in high schools found that all of the 166 reported violent events occurred in locations where there were students but few or no adults

(Astor, Meyer, and Behre 1999). Other school violence studies examining school structural characteristics found large school size and high student/teacher ratios to be predictive of crime and disorder in schools (Duke 1989; Gottfredson and Gottfredson 1985).

Social disorganization theory makes provision for the location and nature of schools. Powerful communities can influence the location and nature of schools. Schools with ample resources are less likely to be overcrowded and will have adequate supervision provided by ample staff (Gottfredson and Gottfredson 1985; Felson 1994). Thus, schools that are organized will be less likely to promote contexts conducive to victimization in neighborhoods around or nearby organized schools. In other words, schools constitute a layer of influence regarding crime on blocks. Schools may be risky places because they bring large numbers of youth into contact with each other. Furthermore, violent crimes can increase if the same number of offenders can find more targets for crime in the absence of a guardian or guardians. In *Crime and Everyday Life* (1994), Felson discusses dangerous places, risky routes, and unassigned space as having the chemistry for crime to occur. Although each crime has its particular chemistry, crimes also have a common chemistry, such as the situation in which clusters of young males with no adults present implies a risk of higher crime of all types (Felson 1994, 42). A key argument that Felson makes is that opportunity for crime will arise not only in and on school grounds, but also nearby and over a larger area (Felson 1987, 921; 1994, 94). Felson's articulation of the flow of offenders and targets with relation to guardianship sets the ground for expansion and integration of theories at a low level of analysis—the block.

SUMMARY

The theoretical and empirical research available to inform theories of place includes three general constructs: physical place, guardianship, and potential offenders. The constructs represent criminal opportunity structures that provide environmental cues as motivation to potential offenders. These environmental cues act collectively to create the circumstances that bring people together, increasing opportunity for offending. Jointly, social disorganization theory, routine activity theory, and defensible space provide guidance for selection of measures to represent the three constructs when studying crime in places. However, the extant literature is limited in its ability to bring together the theories to inform how institutions, such as schools, interact with other social, physical and structural processes and in turn, influence crime. In addition, studies have had limited success approximating the flow of offenders and targets. Most studies utilizing routine activity theory do not attempt to model or measure the ebb and flow of opportunity targets. Studies utilizing new data elements and methods to measure the presence or absence of potential offenders and victims will make important contributions to criminological literature examining neighborhood crime.

Chapter Three

Hypotheses and Data

RESEARCH OBJECTIVE AND HYPOTHESES

The objective of this research is to examine whether, and under what circumstances, schools act as generators of violent crime. This study uses opportunity constructs (integrating social disorganization and routine activity constructs) to examine the relationship between area crime, characteristics of schools, and other neighborhood factors.

To examine neighborhood violent crime, the study develops a model of opportunity factors that is divided into three variable clusters grounded in routine activity theory and social disorganization theory. The variable clusters represent: (1) the risk associated with the physical space or setting, (2) the potential for surveillance or guardianship, and (3) potential for motivated offenders to be present. The first goal is to determine how the opportunity constructs affect violence. Here, the research seeks to answer, "What are the contributions of routine activity and social disorganization constructs to block-level violence?"

With regard to schools, the model for schools consists of opportunity constructs or variable clusters used to characterize schools as unorganized or organized. The cluster of variables associated with schools is, essentially, the elements of physical place risk related to schools. The second goal is to determine whether and how the presence of schools changes any relationship found between violence and opportunity across neighborhoods. The research seeks to answer: "Does a block's proximity to a school influence violence rates on that block?" Similarly, a related goal of this study is to determine whether organized schools affect violence differently than unorganized schools, seeking to answer "Is a block more dangerous when it is close to disorganized school as opposed to an organized school?"

Next, the study determines whether time of day and year adds an important dimension to understanding the relationship of schools to violence across neighborhoods. The related research question is "Given that there are different flows of targets and offenders throughout the day following the routine activities of youth attending school, are there certain time periods when blocks are more dangerous?" The relationship among the variables is examined separately across a series of time periods. Finally, the research seeks to address the interactions between block attributes and school attributes given proximity to schools. The research also examines interaction effects to address the integration of routine activity variables with social disorganization variables.

A general theoretical model is presented in figure 3.1. The ellipses represent the variable clusters that are hypothesized to influence violence. As described later in this chapter, the variable cluster for guardianship can be disaggregated depending on the theory that informs variable selection—either routine activity theory or social disorganization.

The key hypotheses are:

H1. Block-level violent crime rates will be related to exposure to crime as measured by routine activity variables. Violent crime rates will be highest in blocks that have youth hangouts, blocks that have the largest number of busy retail places, blocks with high housing density, and blocks with greater renter crowding.

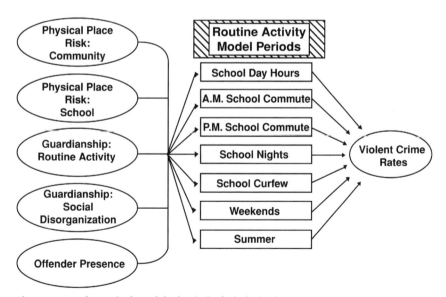

Figure 3.1. Theoretical Model of Criminal Victimization.

H2. Block-level violent crime rates will be related to exposure to crime as measured by neighborhood structural constraints. Violent crime rates will be smallest in blocks characterized by high housing values, high owner-occupancy rates, and low racial and ethnic heterogeneity.

H3. Block-level violent crime rates, will be related to the presence of motivated offenders. Blocks characterized by large number of youth arrestees will be the blocks with the highest rates of violence.

H4. The relationship between violent crime rates and the above opportunity constructs will change with the presence of schools. Blocks close to schools will have higher rates of violence than blocks farther away from schools.

H5. Violent crime rates will be higher for those blocks near schools that have an environment that offers more opportunity for crime. Blocks near low resource schools and schools with a social milieu conducive to violence will experience greater rates of violence.

H6. The above relationships will also be dependent on the time period of the day. Violent crime rates will be greater during periods of time when a large number of people congregate without capable guardians. More specifically, violence will be highest for all person crimes during the school commuting period when youth are less likely to be supervised (less capacity for guardianship). However, as the distance between blocks without schools and blocks with schools increases, violence will decrease in these time periods.

H7. The variations in crime hypothesized above as being related to the routine activities of youth will not necessarily hold true during the summer time. For instance, summer time violent crime rates will not be related to the distance a block is from a school.

RESEARCH SITE

Prince George's County is a large, high-crime county without a large city. The county's 488 square miles surround the District of Columbia along both the District's northeast quadrant and southeast quadrant. The county has the highest crime rates of all Maryland counties, with the exception of Baltimore City. Home to the University of Maryland, half of the county's 767,413 people are black (51 percent), 43 percent are white, 4 percent are Asian, and 4 percent are Hispanic. In 2000, there were 166,860 youth between the ages of 5 and 19. The average household income is roughly $45,000, and 16 percent of households are female-headed (Gaquin and Littman 1999; Maryland Department of Planning 2000).

UNIT OF ANALYSIS

The unit of analysis for this study is the census block. The census block is the entire square physical block, as opposed to two sides of a block facing each other, or a block face (one side of a street bounded by two other streets). The appropriate unit of analysis to better capture the effects of the presence of a school on neighborhood violence is a microlocation, like a block or block face (Sherman, Gartin, and Buerger 1989). In other words, examining particular locations or places become important when studying variation in crime, because the unit of analysis at the microenvironmental level (e.g., blocks, block faces, or block groups) can provide the level of detail needed to capture variation in the independent variables hypothesized to be related to crime. Criminological studies have emphasized that more research at a level of analysis smaller than the census tract is needed to understand the situational and contextual aspects of crime (Brantingham, Dyreson, and Brantingham 1976). Gottfredson (1981) suggests that large-scale surveys and aggregate studies fail to distinguish the characteristics and features of particular areas that are associated with greater risk.

Blocks have regularly recurring rhythms of activity (Jacobs 1961; Taylor 1997b, 1998). Taylor stresses the importance of recognizing streets blocks as "freestanding social, spatial, enduring units in the urban and perhaps suburban residential environments" (1997a, 115). Based on the aforementioned research and other street block research studying social order, control, crime, and decay (Baum et al. 1978; Perkins et al. 1990, Perkins et al. 1992; Roncek 1981; Roncek and Bell 1981; Roncek et al. 1981; Roncek and Faggiani 1985; Roncek and Maier 1991; Roncek and Pravatiner 1989; Taylor, Gottfredson, and Brower 1984; Taylor et al. 1995), the census block is deemed the appropriate level of analysis for this study. Some researchers may argue that it is more appropriate to study the block face. However, because this study examines the domain of youth activity related to attending school, where youth activity is characteristic of individuals walking and cutting through alleys and residential yards, it is feasible to establish that variations in violence will be reflected at the block, not the block face level. Because a block represents multiple block faces and the area in between the block faces, violence that occurs in an alley or an open field would not necessarily be associated with a block face, but would, more accurately, fall within the census block. Furthermore, it has been reported by police departments that crimes that occur at locations that do not have a valid address (like a house or a church) are reported as occurring at the address of the nearest landmark on that block. Hence, attributing an incident to an address on a block face may be misleading, whereas attributing the incident to the entire block is more accurate and hence minimizes measurement error.

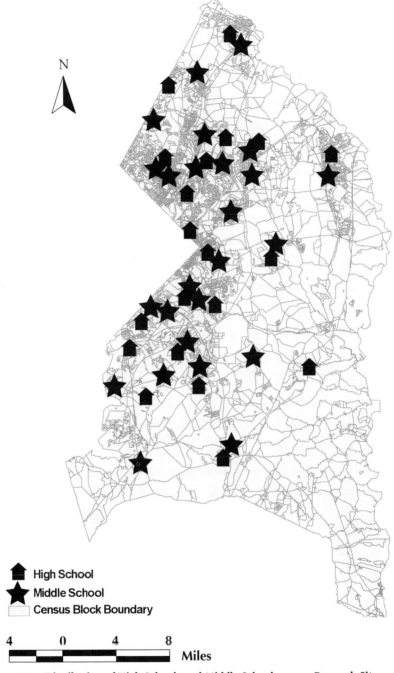

N

High School
Middle School
Census Block Boundary

4   0   4   8
                          Miles

Figure 3.2.   Distribution of High Schools and Middle Schools across Research Site.

According to the U.S. Bureau of the Census (2002), the city block is "a well-defined rectangular piece of land bounded by streets or roads. However, it may be irregular in shape or bounded by railroad tracks, streams, or other features." Prince George's County comprises 7,677 census blocks. Some blocks were extremely small parcels of land comprising less than .00005 square mile. These blocks do not represent streets blocks (too small to contain any activity or have crimes recorded there) and were deleted from the analysis (n=343), leaving 7,334 blocks.

There are 45 middle and high schools spread throughout Prince George's County that were used in this study. All analyses examine the 45 schools as a group, as opposed to examining the effect of middle school versus high schools. Although the two types of schools represent youth of different ages and, perhaps, different behaviors, exploratory analyses indicated that, in many cases, crime was as high around middle schools as it was around high schools. In addition, there were no distinguishing criteria, such as police officers in high schools but not in middle schools that would justify separate analyses. Figure 3.2 shows the distribution of middle and high schools across the county. Elementary schools, vocational schools, schools with under 200 youth (e.g., alternative schools), and specialized schools were excluded from the analysis.

MEASUREMENT OF DEPENDENT VARIABLE

The rate of reported violent crimes per 1,000 population is the dependent variable. Violent crime includes homicide, rape, robbery, aggravated assault, and simple assault. Robberies of commercial establishments are excluded (commercial robberies represented 27.8 percent of all robberies).

Crimes are incident-based data for all person offenses recorded by the Prince George's County Police Department from August 1997 through August 2000. For stability purposes, the victimization data are aggregated using the three-year time period (school years 1997–1998, 1998–1999, 1999–2000). This practice, or using the average of the three years, is standard practice in studies examining aggregate crime across neighborhoods (Roncek and Maier 1991; Smith, Frazee, and Davison 2000). The addresses of victimizations were geocoded in ArcView 3.2 using Streets2000 for Prince George's County, Maryland, as the streets reference file. The reference file (base map) was provided by Geolytics. The map layer was provided without projection and was then projected in Maryland State Plane using a North American Datum (NAD) 83. Geocoding assigns street addresses proportionally along street centerlines based upon street address numeric values. Addresses are offset to the left or right depending on odd or even street numbering. Before geocoding, the data were cleaned for misspellings of addresses using SAS software. After cleaning in SAS, there were 38,244 victimizations to be geocoded. Of the 38,244 victimizations, 36,825 were successfully geocoded for a success rate of 96.3 percent. Victimizations were then summed into census blocks using the spatial join feature of ArcView. Victimizations that occur at intersections that are the boundaries between census blocks cannot be summarized using this process. Of the 36,825 geocoded incidents, 2,794 (7.6 percent) victimizations occurred at intersections of census boundaries. These victimizations were randomly assigned block numbers from the blocks that were part of the intersection.

The appropriate denominator to use when examining crime rates has been the topic of much discussion over the last two and half decades (Bursik and Grasmick 1993; Clarke 1984; Harries 1981; Lynch 1987; Sparks 1980). Most routine activity studies have operationalized the rate of victimization as the number of offenses divided by number of residents or physical structure such as housing units. This study uses the average number of block residents (109), based on U.S. Census data, added to the number of individuals that actually reside in a block to create a population base. The estimated population was then multiplied by three to be used as a denominator for the three-year aggregate of crime. This method takes into account the large number of instances in which crime occurs on blocks where no one resides, and, hence, greatly reduces the skewness of the dependent variable. This technique resulted in a more normal distribution then using the number of structures per block as a measure of population at risk. Moreover, using the number of structures does not adequately represent the population at risk on a block, because victimization opportunity can arise without the presence of structures. Attempts to create population estimates were made using assumptions about the flow of people at different times of day, but insufficient data exist for creating estimates at a low level of aggregation (i.e., the block level). The target site does not keep estimates of daytime or nighttime population, or statistics of resident activity (e.g., population that is employed, population that is retired, etc.) that would assist with creating estimates at the block level. The number of potential targets throughout the day will vary by the routine activities of youth, making it almost impossible to determine a number, representing population at risk, for use in a denominator.

To account for varying victimization risk by time of day this study divides the number of victimizations into periods of the day that correspond to a youth attending school. The time periods examined are: (1) morning school commute, (2) afternoon school commute, (3) school day, (4) school evening/ night, (5) school curfew, (6) weekend, and (7) summertime. Table 3.1 provides a description of the hours used to create the time periods. Some victimizations

Table 3.1.   Time Periods Representing the Routine Activities of Youth.

Time Period	Hours	Hours in Week
School Morning Commute	Mon, Tues, Wed, Thr, Fri 6 a.m. to 9:59 a.m.	20
School Afternoon Commute	Mon, Tues, Wed, Thr, Fri 2 p.m. to 5:59 p.m.	20
School Session/Day	Mon, Tues, Wed, Thr, Fri 10:00 a.m. to 1:59 p.m.	20
School Evening	Sun, Mon, Tues, Wed, Thr 6:00 p.m to 9:59 p.m.	20
School Night Curfew	Sun, Mon, Tues, Wed, Thr 10:00 p.m. to 11:59 p.m.; and Mon, Tues, Wed, Thr, Fri, 12:00 a.m. to 5:59 a.m.	40
Weekend	Friday 6:00 p.m. through 5:59 p.m., Sunday	48

reported to the police span more than one day and over a range of time. These records (1018 or 2.4 percent of the observations) were deleted. Victimizations were divided into time periods and then standardized by population at risk using the formula described above. A limitation of this method is that the same population is used to calculate population at risk in all time periods. However, after exploring the limited number of options, this method was determined to be the least problematic. After creating estimates of population at risk using the average number of residents per block, the distribution of crime rates for each of the time periods remained skewed. This is caused by the large number of blocks that have no crimes. The descriptive statistics for the crime rates are shown in table 3.2. The skewness statistic ranges from six to eleven for crime rates during the different time periods, providing evidence of skewed distributions. To normalize this variable, the variables were transformed using their natural logs. Because the log cannot be taken of zero, 0.01 was added to the crime rates before the variables were transformed. After logging, interpretation of regression coefficients can be expressed as a unit change in an independent variable results in a proportional change in the dependent variable (Cohen and Cohen 1983, 260). The characteristics of the logged variables are shown in table 3.3. The skewness statistic is much closer to zero, indicating more normal distributions.

MEASUREMENT OF INDEPENDENT VARIABLES

This section describes the operationalization of the constructs used in this study to examine crime rates. The measures representing the constructs have been developed from a number of data sources as described in table 3.4. The descriptive statistics for the independent variables are presented in table 3.5. None of the variables is logged.

Table 3.2. Description of Dependent Variables.

Variable	Mean	S.D.	Max	Min	Med	Skew	NMISS	N
Total Victimization Rate, 1997–2000	5.500	13.513	303.581	0	1.822	7.813	0	7334
Total Victimization Rate, School Year, 1997–2000	4.387	10.924	232.153	0	1.039	7.713	0	7334
Total Victimization Rate, Summertime, 1997–2000	1.122	3.410	122.517	0	0.839	11.470	0	7334
Victimization Rate During A.M. School Commute	0.288	1.409	66.677	0	0	20.205	0	7334
Victimization Rate During P.M. School Commute	0.723	2.173	51.998	0	0	8.222	0	7334
Victimization Rate During School Day	0.457	2.310	61.172	0	0	14.718	0	7334
Victimization Rate During School Night	0.741	2.087	38.700	0	0	6.371	0	7334
Victimization Rate During Curfew Hours	0.832	2.875	79.521	0	0	10.660	0	7334
Victimization Rate During Weekend	1.397	4.098	95.248	0	0	8.801	0	7334

Table 3.3. Description of Dependent Variables, Logged.

Variable	Mean	S.D.	Max	Min	Med	Skew	NMISS	N
Total Victimization Rate, 1997–2000	−1.139	3.243	5.716	−4.605	0.600	−0.032	0	7334
Total Victimization Rate, School Year, 1997–2000	−1.445	3.186	5.447	−4.605	0.038	0.108	0	7334
Total Victimization Rate, Summertime, 1997–2000	−3.112	2.535	4.808	−4.605	−4.605	1.169	0	7334
Victimization Rate During A.M. School Commute	−4.034	1.641	4.200	−4.605	−4.605	2.614	0	7334
Victimization Rate During P.M. School Commute	−3.412	2.293	3.901	−4.605	−4.605	1.455	0	7334
Victimization Rate During School Day	−3.876	1.859	4.114	−4.605	−4.605	2.248	0	7334
Victimization Rate During School Night	−3.400	2.308	3.656	−4.605	−4.605	1.446	0	7334
Victimization Rate During Curfew Hours	−3.417	2.316	4.376	−4.605	−4.605	1.499	0	7334
Victimization Rate During Weekend	−2.913	2.663	4.556	−4.605	−4.605	1.001	0	7334

Table 3.4. Constructs, Operationalization, and Data Sources for Block Variables.

Variable	Operationalization/Coding	Data Source
Physical Place Risk		
Youth Hangouts	Dummy variable 1 if block has hangout	PhoneDisc listings, county agencies, telephone validation
Retail Busy Places	Count of restaurants, liquor stores, minimarts, and gas stations	PhoneDisc listings, county liquor board; telephone validation
Guardianship/Routine Activity		
Owner-Occupied	Percentage of housing units that are owner-occupied	U.S. Census 2000
One-Person Households	Percentage of all households that are one-person households	U.S. Census 2000
Housing Density	Number of units per square mile	U.S. Census 2000
Renter Crowding	Percentage of renter-households that contain seven or more people	U.S. Census 2000
Bus Stop Count	Total number of youths at bus stops	Prince George's County Public Schools
Guardianship/Social Disorganization		
Race	Percent of population that is African American	U.S. Census 2000
Racial/Ethnic Hetergeneity	One minus the sum of squared proportions of each of four races: Black, White, Asian, Hispanic	U.S. Census 2000
Female-Headed Households	Percent of households with children headed by a woman	U.S. Census 2000
Economic Well-Being	Median Value Owner Housing	U.S. Census 2000
Distance from Central City	Distance from block centroid to closest border of Washington, D.C., in miles	Calculated using nearest feature extension in ArcView
Offender Presence		
Youth Arrests	Number of all arrests of youth 17 and under 1997–2000 aggregated by location of where arrestee resides	Prince George's County Police Department arrest data
Control Variables		
Block Size		U.S. Census 2000
Prior Victimization	Number of victims aggregated across blocks for 1992–1995	Prince George's County Police Department incident data
Spatial Lag	Neighbors defined as third-order contiguity using Queen criterion (common node)	Created using SpaceStat and ArcView

Table 3.5. Descriptive Statistics.

Variable	Mean	S.D.	Max	Min	Med	Skew	NMISS	N
Physical Place Risk								
Youth Hangouts	0.013	0.115	1.0	0.000	0.000	8.478	0	7334
Retail Busy Places	0.201	0.907	17.00	0.000	0.000	7.324	0	7334
Guardianship-Routine Activities								
Owner-Occupied	69.108	38.330	100.000	0.000	88.890	-1.067	0	7334
One-Person Households	16.413	15.652	100.000	0.000	14.290	1.680	0	7334
Renter Crowding	0.525	2.777	100.000	0.000	0.000	18.057	0	7334
Housing Density	2342.60	4497.3	199709.5	0.000	1682.550	19.649	0	7334
Bus Stop Count, All Day	3.592	15.213	490.000	0.000	0.000	14.546	0	7334
Bus Stop Count, A.M. Commute	1.690	9.871	224.000	0.000	0.000	14.555	0	7334
Bus Stop Count, P.M. Commute	1.823	7.129	238.000	0.000	0.000	13.867	0	7334
Guardianship – Social Disorganization								
African-American	46.595	36.839	100.000	0.000	47.250	0.036	0	7334
Racial Heterogeneity	0.299	0.243	1.000	0.000	0.300	0.116	0	7334
Female Headed Households	6.466	9.251	100.000	0.000	3.850	3.528	0	7334
Median Value Owner Housing	131,620.0	74,995.00	669,000.0	0.000	141,500.0	0.144	0	7334
Distance to D.C.	5.461	4.332	25.760	0.000	4.455	1.1119	0	7334
Offender Presence								
Youth Arrests, 1997–2000	8.269	9.871	234	0.000	0	10.857	0	7334
Controls								
Block Size, in Square Miles	0.066	0.247	5.790	0.000	0.010	10.289	0	7334
Prior Victimization (1992–1995)	5.763	19.749	388.000	0.000	1.000	8.248	0	7334
City	0.768	0.422	1.000	0.000	1.000	-1.267	0	7334
Dummy for Population Zero	0.159	0.366	1.000	0.000	0	1.863	0	7334
School Variables								
Distance to Closest School	1.307	1.545	14.820	0.000	0.960	5.174	0	7334
Resource Deprivation	0.209	0.406	1.000	0.000	0	1.435	0	7334
Disorderly Milieu	0.291	0.454	1.000	0.000	0	0.921	0	7334

Block-Level Explanatory Variables

Physical Place Risk

Block-level physical place risk includes two measures of types of land uses (or places) to denote if blocks have places that provide the opportunity for youth to congregate or particularly attractive places for potential offenders because of accessibility and the presence of people carrying money.

The measures of block-level physical place risk used in this study mirror routine activity variables used in previous small area studies examining the effect of social disorganization and routine activity variables on violence (Smith, Frazee, and Davison 2000). The first variable is a dummy measure to reflect whether blocks have places where youth are likely to populate or "hang out." Hangouts include malls, recreation centers, movie theaters, video arcades, as well as Catholic and private schools. Malls included in this study were the eight largest malls in Prince George's County (LaGrange 1999). Commercial strips and smaller neighborhood malls were not included, because the presence of strip mall stores will most likely be accounted for in other independent measures described below. The data were obtained from PhoneDisc 2000 and validated using government lists of places such as private schools, recreation centers, and malls. There were 114 hangouts across 7,334 blocks. The original intent was to use the number of hangouts as a continuous variable, but the distribution was not suited to regression analysis and therefore, the variable was converted to represent the presence of a youth hang out (value of 1) versus the absence (value of 0). Of the 114 addresses of hangouts, 113 were successfully geocoded.

The second variable is an index that counts all liquor-license establishments (including restaurants), gas stations, and minimarkets. All establishments that serve beer, wine and liquor were included regardless of size or whether alcohol could be carried off the premises. The data were collected using PhoneDisc listings and verified through phone calls. In addition, data on liquor-serving establishments were augmented with a listing of all liquor licenses as of December 2000 provided by Prince George's County Board of License Commissioners. Out of 1,532 establishments, 1,491 (97.3 percent) were successfully geocoded.

Surveillance/Guardianship

These variables are divided into two dimensions: (1) variables that represent guardianship within the routine activity and defensible space framework, and (2) variables that represent guardianship within the framework of social disorganization. However, it is important to recognize, as discussed in chapter 2, that, across the extant literature, the same measures sometimes have been used to represent both theories. The following discussion makes a case for distinguishing between routine activity guardianship and social disorganization guardianship.

Routine Activities/Defensible Space and Guardianship. The first dimension of guardianship is guardianship as implied by housing characteristics that represent ownership, number of residents who would likely be capable guardians, and the number of youth present. Areas where residents take pride in their neighborhoods and show that property is well maintained are more likely to be areas where residents watch over their property and their neighbor's property. Areas with more crowding or groups of youth are less likely to have capable guardians. The variables include the percentage of owner-occupied housing units within a block, the percentage of one-person households, housing density, the percentage of renter households that are overcrowded, and the number of youth using school bus stops. The percentage of owner-occupied housing is the number of owner-occupied housing units per block divided by the number of housing units according to the 2000 U.S. Census. The percentage of one-person households is the number of one-person households divided by the total number of households on that block according to the 2000 U.S. Census. Blocks with larger numbers of one-person households may represent areas that are less guarded because it is likely that the individual is away from the house working and, hence, less people to guard against criminal behavior or the congregation of youth on the block. The percentage of crowded renter households is calculated as the number of renter households with over seven people divided by the total number of renter households. Housing density, another variable derived from 2000 census data, is measured as the number of housing units divided by the size of the block in square miles.

The number of youth using school bus stops is calculated as the total number of youth who used bus stops in December 2000. The variable was calculated from data provided on request by the Prince George's County Public School System. The original data set includes addresses of all school bus stops, the time of day that the bus makes the stop, the number of students picked up or dropped off, and the origin of route and destination. The addresses of bus stops were geocoded using ArcView GIS and then the total stop count per block was calculated. The match rate for geocoding was 95 percent. When bus stops where only one individual was picked up were excluded from the calculation of the match rate, the rate rose to 98 percent, indicating that measurement error from geocoding is most likely minimal.

Social Disorganization and Guardianship. The social disorganization variables used in this study include racial/ethnic heterogeneity, percent black, percentage of female-headed households, median value of owner-occupied housing (as a measure of economic well-being), and distance to Washington,

D.C. With the exception of distance to Washington, D.C., all social disorganization variables were derived using 2000 U.S. Census data.

Racial/ethnic heterogeneity is calculated using the formula $1-\Sigma p_1^2$, where p_1 is the proportion of the total population of the block in a given racial/ethnic group for four groups: white, black, Hispanic, and Asian. This calculation follows neighborhood-level sociological research where communities are made up of more than two racial or ethnic groups (Bellair 1997; Velez 2001; Warner and Roundtree 1997). Values range from zero to one, where low scores indicate blocks that are racially and ethnically homogeneous and high scores represent blocks that are more heterogeneous. Percent black was calculated as the percentage of the total block population who were black alone or part black and some other race. Percentage of households that were headed by females was calculated as the number of households per block headed by females with children present, divided by the total number of households per block.

Block-level census data on median value of owner-occupied housing in 2000 were not available at the time of this study. Although median value data were part of the census short form data available at the block level in 1990, it is not part of the short form data available at the block level in 2000. For this study, the variable was calculated from changes in median housing prices at the block group level between 1990 and 2000 and then estimated for blocks given block median housing values in 1990. Overall, this is a very rough calculation. Measurement error is possible in this calculation because block boundaries changed between 1990 and 2000 and detailed information on how blocks changed with regard to housing units (i.e., the proportion of owner occupied units that changed between census years) was not available to make precise calculations. Alternative block-level variables available in 2000 were examined as possible substitutes to measure economic deprivation (such as percent vacant and abandoned, percent of households that are married), but no strong substitute was found.

The final social disorganization variable is distance to Washington, D.C. This variable represents distance to an urban core. Prince George's County does not have a large city, nor a central city, but Washington, D.C., is a city with a high crime rate and the majority of crime in Prince George's County occurs closer to the D.C. border. The variable is a measure of the distance in miles from every block centroid to the nearest border of Washington, D.C. The variable was created using the Nearest Feature Extension for ArcView.

Offender Presence

Offender presence measures the presence of motivated offenders, one of the three requisites for crime under routine activity theory. This block-level variable is operationalized as the number of all arrests of youth ages 17 and under aggregated for the calendar years 1997 through 2000. It is reasonable to assume that youth arrested (the majority of arrests are for minor crimes, such as trespassing) are not incarcerated for any long periods of crime and hence, the variable captures potential to offend again, rather than capturing a deterrent element. Arrest data were provided by the Prince George's County Police Department and the address provided for each arrest is the home address of the arrestee. There were 25,017 arrests of youth ages 17 and under between 1997 and 2000, and 20,895 were successfully geocoded for a match rate of 84 percent. When those arrests with no address of arrestee provided and arrests of individuals who did not live in Prince George's County were excluded from the match rate, the match rate for geocoding rose to 93 percent. Similar to the dependent variable, data across years were aggregated to achieve stability. Using arrests to measure the presence of motivated offenders represents a significant step forward in an attempt to overcome some of the limitations of past studies in measuring routine activity constructs.

Block-Level Control Variables

The study controls for the size of each block in square miles, because, according to routine activity theory, larger blocks (spaces) are hypothesized to provide more opportunity for offending. Data on block size were obtained from the 2000 U.S. Census.

The study also controls for prior victimization as measured by victimization counts for the calendar year 1992 through 1995. These data were provided by the Prince George's County Police Department. Of 44,525 victimizations, 42,507 were successfully geocoded (95.5 percent).

Spatial Proximity

According to routine activity theory, motivated offenders will commit crimes along the paths that coincide with their routine activities. Crime should occur among frequently used blocks or streets. These frequently used blocks and/or streets will be adjacent to or near each other, literally, because offenders diffuse from where they live to where their daily activities take them. Essentially, then, the amount of crime in one area can be expected to affect the amount of crime in adjacent or nearby areas through diffusion-type processes.

For this study, the potential for crime in one block to be correlated to the crime in a block nearby is modeled as an independent variable, because applications of routine activity theory support its effects (Morenoff and Sampson 1997; Roncek and Montgomery 1995; Smith, Frazee, and Davison 2000). In general, spatial effects can be handled as a nuisance or as a theoretically driven substantive process. Handled as a nuisance, spatial models model spatial dependence in the error terms of the regression model or transform the variables to eliminate spatial correlation. Incorporating spatial dependence as a theoretically explicit variable is referred to as the spatial lag approach (Anselin 1988a, 1989). The lag approach is used in this study with additional efforts to eliminate any remaining spatial error.

Including the spatial lag of violence as an independent variable simultaneously provides (Roncek and Montgomery 1995, 146): (1) a test for spatial autocorrelation, (2) a measure of the effects of spatial autocorrelation on the dependent variable, and (3) adjustments to the effects of all other independent variables. Studies that do not control for crime in one area being affected by crime in surrounding areas have methodological limitations. Without incorporating spatial effects, tests of statistical significance cannot be conducted with validity because of lack of random deviation of the residuals from the predicted values in a regression analysis. Also, if crime in surrounding areas has a causal effect, models will be misspecified, most likely leading to the overestimation of effects for those independent variables in the model. Finally, when using regression techniques, errors of statistical prediction for areas near each other will be correlated, violating one of the assumptions of regression. The spatial lag regression model is defined as:

$$y = \rho Wy + X\beta + \varepsilon,$$

Where y is an N by 1 vector of observations on the dependent variable; Wy is an N by 1 vector composed of elements $\Sigma_i, w_{ij} y_i$, the spatial lags for the dependent variable; ρ is the spatial autoregressive coefficient; X is an N by K matrix of exogenous explanatory variables with an associated K by 1 vector of regression coefficients β; and ε is an N by 1 vector of random error terms, with means 0 and constant (homoskedastic) variances (Anselin 1988a, 1992). The model is often referred to as the simultaneous spatial autoregressive model because the presence of the spatial lag is similar to the inclusion of endogenous variables on the right hand side in systems of simultaneous equations.

In this study, for a given observation I, a spatial lag $\Sigma_i, w_{ij} y_i$ is the weighted average of the crime rates in neighboring locations. The weights matrix used defines neighboring locations as third order contiguity of those block neighbors who share a common node (as opposed to a common border). Essentially this means that for every block, neighbors are all the surrounding (first order) blocks, plus those blocks surrounding the first order neighbors, plus those blocks surrounding the second order neighbors. W_{ij} equals 1 if i and j are contiguous. The spatial autoregressive coefficient ρ represents the effect of a unit change, for a given neighborhood, i, in the average crime rate of the third order neighbors on the crime rate of i.

School-Level Explanatory Variables

A main goal of this study to examine to what extent, and under what conditions, schools act as generators of crime. This study examines a number of variables associated with the presence and characteristics of schools. The school characteristics included in this study are characteristics hypothesized to be related to school disorder and crime. The existing literature that lends itself to the study of crime in or near schools includes studies utilizing school climate theory, defensible space, and social disorganization theory, in which predictors of school disorder include school culture, organizational structure of the schools, the social milieu and the ecological environment (Anderson 1982; Bryk and Driscoll 1988; Gottfredson 2001; Gottfredson and Gottfredson 1985; Toby 1983; Welsh 2000; Welsh, Stokes, and Greene 2000). The literature establishes that schools have their own personalities, similar to individuals.

Characteristics related to school culture include beliefs, attitudes, and values that represent the patterns of interaction among students and staff. School organizational structure refers to the administrative structure of the school, often operationalized using student-teacher ratios, enrollment, level of resources, and classroom size (Gottfredson and Gottfredson 1985; Welsh 2000; Welsh, Stokes, and Greene 2000). The social milieu of a school represents the average characteristics of the student body, such as race, socioeconomic status and percent male. The last dimension of school climate, ecological environment, has been defined using the physical characteristics of the school, such as the age of the buildings, lighting, square footage, number of hallways, and entrances and exits (Short 1990; Toby 1983).

The first school variable analyzes the presence of a school in an area by measuring the distance between every block and the closest school. This variable is the key measure to determine whether schools act as generators of crime. The variable was created by calculating the distance of each block's centroid to the closest school (i.e., the closest block edge containing a school). The calculations were performed using the Nearest Feature Extension for use with ArcView. Blocks with schools are given a zero distance.

The remaining variables represent characteristics of schools. The variables include the percentage of students who failed the Maryland Functional Test in math; the percentage of students who failed the Maryland Functional Test in reading; the percentage of students who failed the Maryland Functional Test in writing; the percentage of students receiving free or reduced-price lunches; the percentage of students absent; percentage of student body that is African American; the size of the student body; the school utilization rate (number of students divided by the state-rated capacity); the number of temporary trailers (modular units) on each school campus; the pupil-teacher (FTE) ratio; and the number of youth arrests per school boundary area standardized by the number of students ("boundary arrests"). This last variable aggregates addresses of all arrests of youth ages 17 and under from 1997 through 2000 into the school boundaries to represent the offender presence construct for each school. Address-level data were provided by the Prince George's County Police Department.[1] School data were obtained from three sources: the U.S. Department of Education's Common Core of School Data, available online, data provided directly by the Prince George's County Public Schools, Office of Research and Evaluation, and data from the Maryland State Department of Education, Maryland School Report Card Assessments. The Common Core of School Data (CCD) are publicly available school-level data on every public school in the United States. Basic school information contained in the CCD include racial composition, school size, type of school and grade levels, and number of students receiving free or reduced lunch. Maryland School Report Card Assessment data are also publicly available and provide information at the school level. These data include number of students absent, number of withdrawals, number of students receiving free and reduced price lunches, and all results of the required Maryland State exams. The data used in this study on percent of students failing exams in reading, writing, and math are the scores from the Grade 9 Functional Test. The percentage of students failing for the Grade 9 Functional Test is reported for every public school. Scores for middle schools (sixth, seventh, and eighth grades) are derived by compiling individual scores for ninth graders and then linked back to the school the individual attended for middle school. School-level variables constructed from the CCD are from the 1998–1999 school year and the remaining school variables are for the 1999–2000 school year. At the time data were collected, CCD data for the 1999–2000 school year were not available. Data on the number of modular units were provided directly by the Prince George's County Public School System.

Bivariate relationships on all school variables were examined to determine the extent of correlation. Table 3.6 provides the correlation matrix. Initially, a racial heterogeneity score for each school was calculated with the intent of including the variable in the factor analysis, but the variable was dropped because it correlated highly with percent black (0.86; p<.0001). To reduce the number of variables used to characterize schools, principal components analysis was used. The correlation analysis confirmed that there were substantial intercorrelations among variables, establishing the feasibility for inclusion in the factor analysis. Principal components analysis (Dunteman 1989) is used to determine how well the variables represent the emerging constructs. Principal components analysis seeks a linear combination of the variables in which the

Table 3.6. Correlation Matrix of School-Level Guardianship Variables.

	Failed Math	Failed Reading	Failed Writing	Pct. Absent	Pct. Reduced Lunch	Pct. Black	Arrests	No. Mods	Enroll-ment	Utili-zation	Pup-FTE
Pct. Failed Math	1.000										
Pct. Failed Reading	.505**	1.000									
Pct. Failing Writing	.667***	.510**	1.00								
Pct. Absent	.331*	.267	0.444**	1.00							
Pct. Reduced Lunch	.149	.173	.027	-.361*	1.00						
Pct. Black	.468**	.218	.52**	0.400**	0.121	1.00					
School Boundary Arrests	0.270	0.164	0.355	-0.128	0.653***	0.232	1.00				
Number of Mods	-0.156	-0.446	-0.110	0.060	-0.32*	-0.146	-0.416**	1.00			
Enrollment	-0.037	0.022	-0.017	0.265	-0.61***	-0.277	-0.561***	0.601***	1.00		
Utilization	-0.065	0.041	-0.122	-0.108	-0.352*	-0.338*	-0.381**	0.537***	0.445**	1.00	
Pupil-FTE Ratio	0.004	-0.057	-0.065	0.132	-0.571	-0.238	-0.375*	0.314*	0.501***	0.589***	1.00

maximum variance is extracted from the variables. After the maximum variance is removed, the analysis seeks a second linear combination that explains the maximum proportion of the remaining variance, and so on. Unlike exploratory factor analysis, principal components analysis makes no assumptions about an underlying causal model and hence is basically a variable reduction strategy (Kim and Mueller 1978; Rummel 1970). The scree plot revealed a major break following factor 2 and eigenvalue for factor 3 was less than one, leading to the conclusion that two factors should be retained. Table 3.7 displays the results of the factor analysis. All variables demonstrate a meaningful loading on either factor 1 or factor 2 (a loading over .40). The factors reflect the school disorder literature. Factor 1 can be seen to represent the amount of resources and related capacity for guardianship. This factor has been named "resource deprivation." Factor 2 reflects the average background characteristics of students. As mentioned earlier, these characteristics have been found to be correlated with increased victimization (Welsh, Stokes, and Greene 2000). This factor has been named "disorderly milieu."

The factor scores for each factor were output as new variables and the distributions were examined. The distributions exhibited a natural break towards the high values for each of the factors. Eight schools had factors scores greater than 0.8 for factor 1, "resource deprivation," and 15 schools scored greater than 0.4 for factor 2, "disorderly milieu." The factor scores were then transformed into dummy variables: those schools with a resource deprivation score larger than 0.8 were given a 1, and all other schools zero; those schools with a milieu score of larger than 0.4 were given a 1 and all other schools

Table 3.7. **Principal Components of Factor Loadings.**

	Factor 1 Resource Deprivation	Factor 2 Disorderly Milieu
Pct Failed Math Functional Test		75
Pct Failed Reading Functional Test		57
Pct Failed Writing Functional Test		83
Pct Free/Reduced Lunch	78	
Percent Absent		59
Percent Black		60
Boundary Arrests	70	
Building Utilization	64	
Pupil Teacher (FTE) Ratio	68	
Number of Modular Units	62	
Actual School Enrollment	81	
Eigenvalue	3.36	2.18

Note: values have been multiplied by 100 and rounded to nearest integer.

zero. These variables were then merged with the variables in the block-level data set. For the resource deprivation factor, all blocks that were closest to schools with factor values of 1 received a 1 (n=1,530). Similarly, all blocks closest to schools with factors values of 1 for disorderly milieu received a 1 (n=2,134).

Data Limitations

One limitation to this study is the use of official police data (incidents records) as a measure of crime. The amount of bias present from using only official police data is unknown. Generally, research has shown that results produced using official records are roughly consistent with results using victimization data (Bastian 1993; Blumstein, Cohen, and Rosenfeld 1991).

Another limitation involves unavailability of data for use in edge correction techniques when conducting spatial analyses. Weights matrices should incorporate measures of crime in blocks outside of Prince George's County that border the county. Incident-based data for 2000 are not available for Washington, D.C., nor are they available for the other counties that border Prince George's County.

Third, the study does not include any variables that measure police presence or any other component of guardianship that is not residential in nature (e.g., based on households and/or residents). Numerous attempts were made to collect police expenditure data, but the data are not available at the block level—or a level remotely close to the block level. District-level data were available, but there are only six districts across 7,334 blocks and the data do not exhibit much variation. Calls for service data (911 emergency calls for service) were examined as a possibility, but the data file only included calls made, not calls cleared by an officer at the scene. Incorporating a strong measure of police presence would strengthen the study by providing a more thorough measurement of the guardianship construct in routine activity theory.

Fourth, the study could be strengthened by adding parcel data. Parcel data provide information on every land parcel, regardless of whether it is commercial, residential or government property. Parcel data can be aggregated by block, providing a strong measure for the number of places. These data may have been able to assist in the calculation of block population at risk. The cost for parcel data for the study site is prohibitive.[2]

Temporal Sequencing

The use of cross sectional data may be problematic in that reverse causation may be operating. In cases of reverse causation, or simultaneous equation bias, the regression estimates will suffer from an upward bias because the estimates will capture the joint impact of both reverse causation and the hypothesized relationship, if there is any. This study tests whether place risk influences victimization but does not specify a model reflecting potential effects of victimization on place risk. Given the nature of the operationalization of constructs for the school variables, reverse causation may not be very probable. School resources and milieu should not be affected by victimization. In the overwhelming majority of cases, these measures should be static over a number of years.

Because reverse causation may be probable at the block level, the study incorporates statistical tests to uncover simultaneous relationships. It is possible that the percentage of owner-occupied housing may be influenced by rates of victimization. Residents, fearing crime, could flee their neighborhoods, causing vacant housing or a larger rental market, thereby influencing levels of owner-occupancy. This hypothesis is tested. The methods used to test for endogeneity are described in detail in chapter 4.

NOTES

1. The school-level arrest data are derived from the same data as the arrest data used at the block level.

2. At the time of data collection, the parcel data base, called MD PropertyView, was available at price of $3,000. The property assessment branch of the State of Maryland suggested I could request information on all parcel addresses needed one at a time, and download the data parcel by parcel. This process would involve making individual requests on over 1 million parcels without knowing the correct address. Obviously, this method was ruled out as being impractical and, perhaps, impossible.

Chapter Four
Analytical Strategy

ANALYTICAL FRAMEWORK

The study tests an opportunity framework developed to examine whether schools act as generators of crime. The study employs ecological data and incident-based crime data to model aggregate patterns of the routine activities of youth. The analysis of criminal victimization focuses specifically on the routine activities of youth attending school, providing the variation needed for a strong study on how the presence of a school effects place risk in terms of violence. Following the daily activities or paths of teenagers can provide better understanding of victimization in and around schools, throughout the school day and school year. Because offenders generally commit their offenses near places where they spend most of their time (Brantingham and Brantingham 1991; Cohen and Felson 1979), it can easily be reasoned that youth offenders commit a portion of their offenses near schools or on pathways to and from school. Restricting the scope of inquiry to one specific domain of life activity can increase the explanatory power of activity models, and at the same time provide useful information that might lead to specific solutions to crime problems (Lynch 1987). It can be reasoned from routine activity theory that diffusion of youth along paths can take a number of forms, and does not necessarily adhere to a contagion model. Youth may leave school and move to another area that is not contiguous with the school. The variables included in this study are consistent with other models of activity diffusion. Youth meeting at school may seek out potential targets not on the *physical paths* to or from school. The models tested are designed to capture other features of the environment that create the opportunity for violence (e.g., youth hangouts, crowded housing areas, etc.). Furthermore, incorporating time of day into the models will assist with understanding potentially different activity patterns.

The research examines different time periods that coincide with different activities of youth attending school (one domain), because the author believes that the activities associated with the time of day and time of year related to the routines of attending school—school session, school commute, evening, weekends, and summertime versus school year—influence the number of offenders, targets, and guardians that are available. Essentially, this study examines measures of offender and target flow as well as the environmental cues that create opportunity contexts for violent crime.

The study views schools as microenvironments which vary along a host of situational and environmental dimensions that are important to modeling the risk of victimization. This study follows the analytical strategy of recent research (Morenoff, Sampson, and Raudenbush 2001; Sampson and Raudenbush 1999; Smith, Frazee, and Davidson 2000) seeking to understand how places fare in terms of guardianship and risk of victimization—without focusing on the production of offenders but, instead, focusing on the context or place.

With regard to examining violence using a routine activity framework, this study follows the analytical strategy used by Lynch (1987) to examine only one domain of life activity—the school domain. Analysis of incident-based data and victimization survey data have shown that the risk of violence against youth varies greatly by time of day (Snyder 1999; Wiebe and Meeker 1998). Thus, understanding the factors associated with crime at different times of day is critical. Previous research conducted in Washington, D.C., by the author found that youth victimization patterns are more easily detected when victimization is aggregated by time periods related to the routine activities of attending school (e.g., school day, after-school period, etc.). The hourly rate of victimization was higher during the school commute than during any other time period, followed by weekend night and school session periods. Youth victimization patterns changed during the summer months (Gouvis et al. 2001; Gouvis, Johnson, and Roth 1997). Whether school is in session (time of year, or nonschool weeks) changes crime patterns. Examining South Carolina incident based data on youth, McManus (2001) found that for violent gun crimes that happened in school or on school grounds, the crimes were most common on weekdays when school was in session from 6 p.m. to 9 p.m. When school was not in session, violent crime incidents occurred later in the evening and with more frequency on weekends. Research has also confirmed that patterns of crime are different depending on the school activity in which the youth is participating. An examination of youth victim narratives from a 1982–1983 sample from the NCVS found that students were more often victims of a violent crime while traveling to and from school or waiting for a school bus (Garofalo, Siegel, and Laub 1987) then when in the classroom during the day. A recent study published in the *American Educational Research Journal* (Astor, Meyer, and Behre 1999) stressed the importance of understanding how violence within high schools interacted with specific locations and times but did not take into account the physical or social characteristics of the area immediately surrounding the schools in their research.

Routine activity theory is useful in understanding why violence might vary over different times of the day. As the number of potential targets increase (holding constant the presence of motivated offenders and absence of capable guardians), the opportunity for victimization increases. Hence, as the flow of youth changes, so too may the incidence of violent crime. However, measuring the number of potential targets available across different times of the day was not possible for this study. Block-level population approximations at any given time of day are not available and are beyond the scope of this study. Because residents are engaging in their routine activities—going to work, school, leisure activities—throughout the day, the number of targets does not always equal the number of residents living in a block, census tract, neighborhood, and so forth. It would be ideal to have a direct measure of the extent of potential targets at different times of the day. Given the difficulty of calculating or even estimating these numbers, this study breaks down the day into time periods as a proxy for the differing flows of youth.

Instrumental Variables Estimation

Regression analysis is appropriate for this study because the intent is to determine which of several independent variables are important for describing or predicting victimization risk. Also, with regression analyses, separate models can be used to compare several derived regression relationships (Kleinbaum and Kupper 1978).

Models are estimated by means of instrumental variables (IV) methods. Ordinary Least Squares regression (OLS) is not appropriate because the OLS estimator will be biased as well as inconsistent for the parameters of the spatial model. The multidirectional nature of the spatial dependence limits the type of statistical procedures that will lead to consistent estimates. Essentially, the breakdown of OLS in models with spatially lagged dependent variables is due to the correlation between the spatial variable and the error term. This problem is similar to the estimation of parameters in a system of simultaneous equations, where the dependence between endogenous variables and error terms is at issue in OLS (Anselin 1988a: 82). IV methods are a robust alternative to maximum likelihood estimation. Maximum likelihood estimation (MLE) cannot be used in this study because SpaceStat cannot, nor is other software available to, create a full weights matrix needed for MLE. The dataset contains over 7,000 observations, making the creation of a full weights matrix impossible. Although instrumental variables estimation for models with spatial dependence has not often been applied in criminological studies, it has been shown to be functional (Anselin 1984, 1988a). A benefit of IV estimation is that the assumption of normally distributed error terms is not needed.

Instrumental variables estimation is based on the principle that a set of instruments, Q, are strongly correlated with the original variables, Z, but asymptotically uncorrelated with the error term. After identification of instruments, the instruments are used to construct a proxy for the endogenous variables, which consists of their predicted values in the regression on the instruments and the exogenous variables. The proxy variable can then be used in least squares regression.

There exists little formal guidance in the selection of instruments for the spatially lagged variable. A requirement for selection is that the instrument and the existing variable are asymptotically uncorrelated. Anselin (1980) suggests that the use of the spatial lags of the exogenous variables will provide satisfactory results. Following Anselin's suggestion, the lags of all exogenous variables were used as instruments in regression equations. All models are run using SpaceStat software Version 1.91 (Anselin 1992).

Regression Diagnostics: Testing for Spatial Autocorrelation

Instrumental variables estimation is used in this study because crime rates are spatially autocorrelated. The SpaceStat software is used to run regressions with diagnostics for spatial effects. Four tests for spatial dependence can be utilized to determine the nature and extent of spatial dependence. Because the data used for this study originally exhibited non-normal error terms, a test robust against non-normal error is used. This test, the Kelejian Robinson test (1992), does not require normality for the error terms. The test is a large sample test that follows a χ^2 distribution with P degrees of freedom. To test for spatial lag (as opposed to spatial error), Anselin suggests using the Lagrange Multiplier (LM) diagnostic (Anselin 1988b). The LM test also follows a χ^2 distribution with 1 degree of freedom. These tests are used and reveal the presence of spatial lag. Tests were run on all base models to determine the extent and nature of spatial dependence. Both the Lagrange Multiplier test for spatial lag and the Kelejian-Robinson test were significant, suggesting the presence of both error and lag (For base school year model: LM=36, p<.0001; Kelejian-Robinson=382, p<.0001)

In addition to tests for spatial autocorrelation, tests for multicollinearity, normal error distribution and heteroskedasticity were also conducted. With regard to multicollinearity, SpaceStat calculates a "condition number" (Belsley, Kuh, and Welsch 1980). Values of the condition number larger than 30 are considered to be problematic. For this study, all models run with the exception of the models containing interactions have condition numbers between 7 and 12. The final models containing interactions have conditions numbers ranging from 20 to 25. Because these numbers are close to 30 and, hence, suggest multicollinearity, additional diagnostics were conducted. SAS was used to calculate the variable inflation factors (VIF) for each of the variables. All variables had VIF scores under 10, suggesting that multicollinearity should not be an issue in the regression results.

Tests for nonnormal errors were conducted using an asymptotic test suggested by Kiefer and Salmon (1983). The tests revealed nonnormal error. Nonnormal error suggests that care must be taken in interpreting the coefficients. Heteroskedasticity was examined using the Breusch-Pagan (BP) test (Breusch and Pagan 1979) and the Koenker-Basset statistic. The Koenker-Bassett is used when normality has been rejected. Diagnostic tests using the interactive mapping feature between SpaceStat and ArcView revealed that adding a categorical variable distinguishing the west side of the county from the east side of the county should control heteroskedasticity. Hence, all instrumental variables models are run using the Groupwise heterogeneity (GHET) approach. This groupwise procedure utilizes the categorical variable to set up regimes or groups of observations, allowing for some from of heteroskedasticity. The different group variances are treated as "nuisance parameters" and, thus, no standard errors (or t-tests, etc.) are computed (Anselin 1988a, 80).

Alternative methods for analyzing the data could include using a negative binomial regression model to examine the theoretical model in which the dependent variable (crime) is the count of crime in blocks. However, software that can handle overdispersed Poisson variates and spatial dependence is very limited and has rarely been utilized in the study of criminology. Negative binomial regression is a Poisson-based regression model that allows for overdispersion — when count variables have variances greater than the mean. Linear regression models with count variables can result in inefficient, inconsistent and biased estimates (Cameron and Trivedi 1998; Liao 1994; Long 1997). The majority of blocks in the study site have zero crimes, which essentially is a truncation of the dependent variable. This truncation renders OLS estimates biased and inconsistent. Negative binomial regression models can account for the large number of zeros. Given the limited availability of spatial Poisson models, this study transforms the dependent variable into rates and uses instrumental variables regression within a spatial framework.

Estimation of Regression Models

For this study, four sets of models are tested. The main model tested is as follows:

CRIMERATE DURING SCHOOL YEAR= place risk(liqmart, hang_dum), RA/ guardianship(bussed, hudens, pctrcrd, pct1per, ownocc), SD/guardianship (racehet, pctfemh, pctblack, hmval, dist_dcm), offender presence, convic, sqmile, spatiallag

The second set of models that are run are similar to the above, but include the school variables: each block's distance to the nearest middle or high school, resource deprivation and disorderly milieu. The third set of models run are the same as the models above, but the victimization rate is disaggregated by time of day. Models are run for each of the six time periods (school morning commute, afternoon school commute, school session, curfew, weekends, and weekday evening). In addition, a model regressing summertime crime rates on place risk, guardianship, and offender presence is tested.

The last set of models run includes interaction effects between the social disorganization variables and the routine activity variables. Five relationships are hypothesized:

H8. The effect of busy places on violence will only be strong in socially disorganized areas as measured by low housing values.

H9. As the distance between blocks and schools increases, the strength of the effect of a block containing a youth hangout on violence will decrease.

H10. As the distance between blocks and schools increases, the strength of the effect of the number of retail busy places on violence will decrease.

H11. As the percentage of female-headed households increases, the criminogenic effect of high housing density will increase.

H12. The effect of the presence of motivated offenders (youth arrestees) on violence will be larger in areas where there are high percentages of female-headed households.

Testing for Simultaneous Relationships

Before the models are estimated using instrumental variables regression, tests for the presence of endogenous regressors are undertaken. Using theory as a guide, one can plausibly argue that owner-occupancy rates may be influenced by crime. Again using theory as a guide, the percentage of households that are occupied by married couples is used as an instrument. This variable correlates strongly with owner occupancy (0.753, p<0.0001) and does not correlate strongly with violent crime (0.034, p=0.004). Similarly, in a model regressing all exogenous variables on owner occupancy, percentage of married households is the strongest predictor. Using the SAS procedure Proc REG revealed a standardized estimate of .307 for percentage of married households, compared to estimates of other variables that ranged from 0.010 to 0.250. The Hausman specification test (Hausman 1978) in SAS Proc Model is used to determine whether an instrumental variables method is needed to estimate the study models (null hypothesis of the test is that there is no simultaneity). The Hausman statistic derived is 5.93 with an associated 0.994 probability, indicating that instrumental variables methods are not needed for the study models.

Chapter Five

Research Findings

CORRELATIONS

Variable correlations are shown in table 5.1. Most variables are not highly correlated. The strongest bivariate positive relationship occurs between the variables percent African American and percent owner occupied (.43; p<.001). This is surprising in light of the research literature, and particularly, social disorganization theory, that suggests that the number of African Americans is associated with economic disadvantage and hence limited owner-occupancy. It may be that Prince George's County is enticing to Washington, D.C., African Americans who are looking to purchase a home but cannot afford to buy a home in the District. Minority populations other than African Americans may be more likely to rent. A moderate correlation is found between percent African Americans and percent female-headed households (.40; p<.001). This finding is consistent with the literature (Bursik and Grasmick 1989; Smith, Frazee, and Davison 2000). Also consistent with social disorganization theory, the negative correlation between percent African American and distance from central city (the District of Columbia) (-.38, p<.001) indicates that as one moves further east away from the District, the percentage of residents who are African American decreases. Not surprisingly, violent crime rates in an earlier time period are moderately correlated with current violent crime rates (.35; p<.001). In general, the findings from the correlation analysis are consistent with the literature.

INSTRUMENTAL VARIABLES REGRESSION RESULTS

As stated in the previous chapter, analysis of the relationship between violent crime rates and place risk, guardianship, and offender presence is estimated

Table 5.1. Correlation Coefficients of Variables (N=7,334).

	1	2	3	4	5	6	7	8
1	1.00							
2	0.10***	1.00						
3	0.25***	0.24***	1.00					
4	0.06***	-0.05***	-0.15***	1.00				
5	0.11***	0.03*	0.03**	0.20***	1.00			
6	0.09***	0.01	0.03*	-0.06***	-0.00	1.00		
7	0.15***	0.07***	0.12***	0.02*	0.04***	0.01	1.00	
8	0.11***	-0.02*	-0.04***	-0.01	0.24***	0.04***	-0.02*	1.00
9	0.32**	0.02	-0.02	0.43***	0.22***	0.06***	0.10***	0.21***
10	0.08***	0.00	-0.01	0.42***	0.24***	0.05***	0.04***	0.15***
11	0.21***	0.04***	0.03*	0.08***	0.11***	0.07***	0.07***	0.22***
12	0.19***	0.00	-0.05***	0.15***	-0.14***	-0.05***	0.02	-0.16***
13	0.29***	0.02	-0.04**	-0.06***	-0.11***	-0.05***	-0.02	-0.12***
14	0.25***	0.08***	0.10***	-0.08***	0.09***	0.07***	0.21***	0.20***
15	0.10***	0.08***	0.10***	0.01	0.01	-0.01	0.22***	-0.10***
16	0.35***	0.18***	0.42***	-0.18***	0.10***	0.08***	0.30***	0.13***

	9	10	11	12	13	14	15	16
1								
2								
3								
4								
5								
6								
7								
8								
9	1.00							
10	0.05***	1.00						
11	0.40***	0.07***	1.00					
12	-0.24***	0.04**	-0.23***	1.00				
13	-0.38***	-0.04***	-0.19***	0.36***	1.00			
14	0.18***	0.02*	0.23***	-0.09***	-0.09***	1.00		
15	-0.03**	0.04**	-0.03**	0.16***	0.18***	0.07***	1.00	
16	0.16***	-0.03**	0.23***	-0.12***	-0.16***	0.61***	0.09***	1.00

Key
1. School Year Violent Crime Rate
2. Youth Hangout Dummy
3. Retail Busy Places
4. Pct. Owner Occupied
5. Pct One-Person Household
6. Pct. Renter Crowding
7. Bus Stop Count
8. Housing Density
9. Pct. African Americans
10. Racial Heterogeneity
11. Pct. Female-Headed Households
12. Median Value Housing
13. Distance from City
14. Youth Arrests
15. Block Size
16. Prior Victimization Levels

p<.05; *p<.01; ***p<.001.

using instrumental variables. All 7,334 census blocks were included in the analysis. Blocks with zero housing units (n=1,136) were not removed from the models because elimination of these blocks would exclude an important type of place from the analysis. Theoretically, it remains vital to assess the effects of unpopulated areas. Values for variables such as percent owner occupancy and percent female-headed households in unpopulated blocks are zero. This technique keeps all observations in the model. A dummy variable is included (1=no housing units) to capture the effects of the zero-value variables.

Table 5.2 shows the findings that address the fundamental research hypotheses described in chapter 3. Specifically, table 5.2 addresses hypothesis one. The table includes two pseudo R^2 measures. The traditional R^2 measures of fit are not appropriate when using an instrumental variables approach. The

Table 5.2.   Instrumental Variables Regression of the Log of Violent Crime Rates on Place Risk, Guardianship, and Offender Presence, School Year, 2000.

Variables	Base Model-School Year
Place Risk	
Presence of Youth Hangout	0.507*
Number of Busy Retail Places	0.572**
Guardianship-Routine Activity	
Pct. Owner-Occupied	−0.006**
Pct. One-Person Households	−0.003
Pct. Renter Crowding	0.035**
Bus Stop Count	0.007***
Housing Density[†]	0.002
Guardianship-Social Disorganization	
Pct. African Americans	0.009***
Racial Heterogeneity	0.700***
Pct. Female Headed Households	0.006
Median Value Owner Housing[†]	−0.003***
Distance from City	−0.051***
Offender Presence	
Youth Arrests	0.021***
Control Variables	
Block Size	1.230***
Prior Victimization	0.019***
Zero Population	−1.560***
Spatial Lag	0.485***
Constant	−0.549*
R^2	0.28
Sq. Corr.	0.28
Lagrange Multiplier (error)	9.681**
N	7,334.000

* p<0.05; **p<0.01; ***p<0.001.
[†]Coefficients for variable have been multiplied by 1,000.

R^2 reported in the tables is the ratio of the variance of the predicted values over the variance of the observed values for the dependent variables. The second measure is the squared correlation. This is the square correlation between the predicted and observed values.

With regard to the individual model coefficients, the significance of these parameters is based on the standard normal distribution and not, as is the case in OLS, the Student t distribution. SpaceStat computes an asymptotic t-test as the ratio of the estimate to its asympototic standard error (Anselin 1992).

The model shown in table 5.2 regresses school year violent crime rates on place risk, guardianship, offender presence, and the control variables. All models include the spatial lag. All variables are significant with the exception of renter crowding, one-person households, and housing density indicating support for the hypothesis that place risk, guardianship, and offender presence influence opportunity for violent crime. The only diagnostic SpaceStat provides at this time is an asymptotic Lagrange Multiplier (LM) test for remaining spatial error autocorrelation. This test takes into account the spatial lag as an endogenous regressor. The LM test for error reveals some significant spatial error remains (LM=9.681, p<.01). To address this remaining spatial error, the remaining models are estimated with groupwise heteroskedasticity. The heteroskedastic parameters are treated as nuisance parameters and therefore, no inference is possible. During earlier examination of data, basic dynamic exploratory spatial data analysis tools (ESDA) were used to explore spatial heterogeneity. Maps revealed that blocks on the west side of the county, closer to Washington, D.C., exhibited high spatial autocorrelation—blocks of high crime were surrounded by blocks of high crime. The patterns of autocorrelation were different for blocks on the east side. Because of this pattern, a new variable was created to capture these differences. Blocks on the greater west side of the county were given a value of 1 for the new "city" variable (n=5,629).

The same model examining school year violent crime rates was reestimated using the IV-groupwise heterogeneity (GHET) procedure in SpaceStat. The results are shown in table 5.3. The estimates of the coefficients are generally similar to those derived without the GHET procedure (table 5.2). Some significance levels change and one variable that was significant when heteroskedasticity was not modeled—percentage of female-headed households—no longer has a significant relationship with violent crime rates.

The coefficients cannot be interpreted as a one-unit change in the independent variable produces a corresponding one-unit change in the dependent variable because the dependent variable has been transformed into its natural log. The independent variables are not in log form. This type of model is often referred to as a log-linear model. As stated earlier, the slope

Table 5.3.   Instrumental Variables Regression with GHET of the Log of Violent Crime Rates on Place Risk, Guardianship, and Offender Presence, School Year, 2000.

Variables	Base Model-School Year
Place Risk	
Presence of Youth Hangout	0.534***
Number of Busy Retail Places	0.577**
Guardianship- Routine Activity	
Pct. Owner-Occupied	−0.006**
Pct. One-Person Households	−0.003
Pct. Renter Crowding	0.034**
Bus Stop Count	0.007**
Housing Density[†]	0.002
Guardianship-Social Disorganization	
Pct. African Americans	0.009***
Racial Heterogeneity	0.721***
Pct. Female Headed Households	0.007**
Median Value Owner Housing[†]	−0.003***
Distance from City	−0.052***
Offender Presence	
Youth Arrests	0.022***
Control Variables	
Block Size	1.213***
Prior Victimization	0.019***
Zero Population	−1.524***
Spatial Lag	0.473***
Constant	−0.618**
East Side	6.271***
West Side	7.663***
R^2	0.28
Sq. Corr.	0.28
N	7,334.000

* $p<0.05$; **$p<0.01$; ***$p<0.001$.
[†]Coefficients for variable have been multiplied by 1,000.

measures the proportional or relative change in the dependent variable given an absolute change of one unit of the independent variable. For ease of interpretation, multiplying the coefficient by 100 provides the percentage change in the crime rate for an absolute change of one unit of the independent variable.

Both place risk variables are significant. Blocks that have youth hangouts increase violent crime by 53 percent. In addition, every liquor store, restaurant, minimart, or gas station increases violent crime by 58 percent. Looking at the guardianship variables, a 10 percent increase in owner-occupancy reduces violent crime by 6 percent, and every additional ten youth congregating at bus stops increases violence by 7 percent. Overcrowded blocks with regard to renter housing are also associated with increases in crime. All the social disorganization/guardianship variables are highly significant in the expected direction. Blocks with higher percentages of African Americans experience more violence. A 10 percent increase in African American residents is associated with a 9 percent increase in violence. Similarly, a 10 percent increase in female-headed households is associated with a 7 percent increase in violence. A $1,000 increase in median housing price results in a 2 percent decrease in the violent crime rate. The coefficient for racial heterogeneity is very large (0.721). Blocks that have total racial heterogeneity experience 72 percent more violence than those blocks that are completely homogeneous. Blocks further from Washington, D.C., have lower violent crime rates; every additional mile from the District is associated with a 5 percent decrease in violence.

As discussed in earlier chapters, the youth arrests variable represents the presence of potential motivated offenders. This variable is a significant predictor of violent crime. An additional ten arrests within a block increases the violent crime rate twenty percent. This is an important finding in light of the absence of studies to incorporate measures of potential offending. Furthermore, the criminological literature has shown that areas with large numbers of arrests may have lower crime rates because arrests can act as a deterrent to crime (Blumstein, Cohen, and Nagin 1978; Logan 1975; Marvell and Moody 1996; Sampson and Cohen 1988; Wilson and Borland 1978).

As expected, the control variables are significant. Larger blocks are associated with increases in crime, and prior violent crime rates predict current violent crime rates. Also as expected the coefficient for the spatial lag is significant, demonstrating that the spatial lag model is appropriate for the data. The significance of the groupwise heterogeneity variable "city" also indicates that the GHET procedure is necessary to capture any remaining spatial error.

In general the findings from table 5.3 support the hypotheses that social disorganization and opportunity as defined by routine activity theory influence crime. This finding is only one part of a multipart study to examine how opportunity influences crime.

The result of the instrumental variables regression (GHET) for summertime violent crime rates is shown in table 5.4. The variables included in the model are the same as those in the school year model, with the exception of the exclusion of the bus stop count variable. Because the summer would not have youth congregating at school bus stops, this variable is not included in the model of summertime violence. The coefficients and their significance are generally similar to those in the model of school year violence. The effect of the place risk variables do not change very much between the two time periods.

Table 5.4. Instrumental Variables Regression with GHET of the Log of Violent Crime Rates on Place Risk, Guardianship, and Offender Presence, Summer, 2000.

Variables	Base Model-Summer
Place Risk	
Presence of Youth Hangout	0.506**
Number of Busy Retail Places	0.482***
Guardianship- Routine Activity	
Pct. Owner-Occupied	−0.007***
Pct. One-Person Households	−0.000
Pct. Renter Crowding	0.005
Bus Stop Count	———
Housing Density[†]	0.006
Guardianship-Social Disorganization	
Pct. African Americans	0.006***
Racial Heterogeneity	0.313**
Pct. Female Headed Households	0.011**
Median Value Owner Housing[†]	−0.001**
Distance from City	−0.024**
Offender Presence	
Youth Arrests	0.017***
Control Variables	
Block Size	0.904***
Prior Victimization	0.027***
Zero Population	−0.741**
Spatial Lag	0.307***
Constant	−2.153***
East Side	3.508***
West Side	5.287***
R^2	0.25
Sq. Corr.	0.24
N	7,334.000

* $p<0.05$; ** $p<0.01$; *** $p<0.001$.
[†]Coefficients as shown for variable have been multiplied by 1,000.

There are a few notable differences between the model results. Housing density predicts violent crime during the summertime, but not during the school year. This makes intuitive sense in that the routines of youth are more neighborhood oriented during the summer when youth are either working or engaged in leisure activities. However, to the contrary, Tables 5.3 and 5.4 show that there is a significant effect of renter crowding on violent crime during the school year but not in the summer. Following that housing density is significant during the summer may lead one to hypothesize that renter crowding, then, would also be an important variable during the summer. The R^2 for each model reveals that the school year model generally fits the data better than for the summertime model (.28 versus .25).

Results of Regression Models Incorporating Time of Day

Tables 5.5 through 5.10 show the results of the models that examine crime during different periods of the day and week. The models are morning school commute, afternoon school commute, school session, school night, curfew, and weekend, respectively. Regression results for the morning school commute are shown in table 5.5. The findings indicate that the presence of a youth hangout does not influence crime during the morning commute, though the presence of busy retail establishments increases crime. Not surprisingly, retail busy establishments have a much smaller effect on morning crime than they do on crimes across the entire 24-hour period (table 5.3). Of the guardianship variables, only owner occupied, bus stop count, African American, housing values, and distance

Table 5.5. Instrumental Variables Regression with GHET of the Log of Violent Crime Rates on Place Risk, Guardianship, and Offender Presence, A.M. Commute, 2000.

Variables	A.M. Commute
Place Risk	
Presence of Youth Hangout	0.167
Number of Busy Retail Places	0.081***
Guardianship-Routine Activity	
Pct. Owner-Occupied	−0.002**
Pct. One-Person Households	0.001
Pct. Renter Crowding	0.007
Bus Stop Count (morning count)	0.012***
Housing Density†	0.002
Guardianship-Social Disorganization	
Pct. African Americans	0.002***
Racial Heterogeneity	0.048
Pct. Female Headed Households	0.002
Median Value Owner Housing†	−0.001**
Distance from City	−0.017**
Offender Presence	
Youth Arrests	0.006**
Control Variables	
Block Size	0.268***
Prior Victimization	0.025***
Zero Population	−0.247*
Spatial Lag	0.147**
Constant	−3.473***
East Side	1.137***
West Side	2.505***
R^2	0.19
Sq. Corr.	0.19
N	7,334.000

* $p<0.05$; ** $p<0.01$; *** $p<0.001$.
†Coefficients for variable have been multiplied by 1,000.

Table 5.6.   Instrumental Variables Regression with GHET of the Log of Violent Crime Rates on Place Risk, Guardianship, and Offender Presence, P.M. Commute, 2000.

Variables	P.M. Commute
Place Risk	
Presence of Youth Hangout	0.634**
Number of Busy Retail Places	0.351***
Guardianship-Routine Activity	
Pct. Owner-Occupied	−0.004***
Pct. One-Person Households	−0.001
Pct. Renter Crowding	0.009
Bus Stop Count (After school count)	0.017***
Housing Density[†]	−0.003
Guardianship-Social Disorganization	
Pct. African Americans	0.004***
Racial Heterogeneity	0.139
Pct. Female Headed Households	0.008**
Median Value Owner Housing[†]	−0.001**
Distance from City	−0.028***
Offender Presence	
Youth Arrests	0.020***
Control Variables	
Block Size	0.466***
Prior Victimization	0.025***
Zero Population	−0.656***
Spatial Lag	0.284***
Constant	−2.343***
East Side	2.464***
West Side	4.553***
R^2	0.23
Sq. Corr.	0.23
N	7,334.000

* $p<0.05$; ** $p<0.01$; *** $p<0.001$.
[†]Coefficients for variable have been multiplied by 1,000.

from a central city are significant. The number of youth arrests has a significant effect on violent crime, and the control variables remain significant. Table 5.6 shows the results of the regression examining the after school period. As discussed in chapter 3, it is hypothesized that youth hangouts and retail busy places would have a strong effect on violence. The findings support the hypothesis. The presence of a youth hangout increases the violent crime rate 63 percent and every retail busy place increases violent crime 35 percent. The percentage of African Americans, female-headed households, and housing values are all significant, as is the distance a block is from a city. The presence of motivated offenders as measured by youth arrests exhibits a stronger relationship on violence during the after-school commute period than during the morning commute. This finding is supported by routine activity theory, which states that

Table 5.7. Instrumental Variables Regression with GHET of the Log of Violent Crime Rates on Place Risk, Guardianship, and Offender Presence, School Session, 2000.

Variables	School Session
Place Risk	
Presence of Youth Hangout	0.511**
Number of Busy Retail Places	0.247***
Guardianship-Routine Activity	
Pct. Owner-Occupied	−0.004***
Pct. One-Person Households	−0.001
Pct. Renter Crowding	−0.001
Bus Stop Count	—
Housing Density[†]	−0.004
Guardianship-Social Disorganization	
Pct. African Americans	0.002**
Racial Heterogeneity	0.165**
Pct. Female Headed Households	0.003
Median Value Owner Housing[†]	−0.0002
Distance from City	−0.020***
Offender Presence	
Youth Arrests	0.009***
Control Variables	
Block Size	0.457***
Prior Victimization	0.029***
Zero Population	−0.336**
Spatial Lag	0.149**
Constant	−3.310***
East Side	1.629***
West Side	3.004***
R^2	0.23
Sq. Corr.	0.22
N	7,334.000

* $p<0.05$; ** $p<0.01$; *** $p<0.001$.
[†]Coefficients for variable have been multiplied by 1,000.

periods of reduced supervision will have more crime. The after-school period is a time of day characterized by youth attending sports activities or engaged in other leisure activities not necessarily with strong supervision. During the morning period, youth have a singular destination—school—a place and time where youth are required to go, unlike the after-school period.

Table 5.7 shows the findings of the regression of school session violence on the independent variables. Youth hangouts and retail busy places both exhibit criminogenic effects, but neither effect is as strong as the effect of these establishments during the after-school period. Percentage of female-headed households is not significant, nor is median housing values; both influenced crime during the after school commute. With the exception of percentage owner-occupied, none of the other housing variables is significant. Racially

Table 5.8. Instrumental Variables Regression with GHET of the Log of Violent Crime Rates on Place Risk, Guardianship, and Offender Presence, School Night, 2000.

Variables	School Night
Place Risk	
Presence of Youth Hangout	0.407**
Number of Busy Retail Places	0.389***
Guardianship-Routine Activity	
Pct. Owner-Occupied	−0.005***
Pct. One-Person Households	−0.002
Pct. Renter Crowding	−0.009
Bus Stop Count	—
Housing Density[†]	0.012*
Guardianship-Social Disorganization	
Pct. African Americans	0.005***
Racial Heterogeneity	0.163
Pct. Female Headed Households	0.007**
Median Value Owner Housing[†]	−0.001**
Distance from City	−0.017**
Offender Presence	
Youth Arrests	0.022***
Control Variables	
Block Size	0.625***
Prior Victimization	0.025***
Zero Population	−0.724***
Spatial Lag	0.308***
Constant	−2.332***
East Side	2.692***
West Side	4.491***
R^2	0.24
Sq. Corr.	0.24
N	7,334.000

* $p<0.05$; ** $p<0.01$; *** $p<0.001$.
[†]Coefficients for variable have been multiplied by 1,000.

heterogeneous blocks have a small effect on crime, and, as in previous models, distance from the District of Columbia has an effect on crime. Youth arrests have a significant effect on crime, though, as expected, the effect is smaller than during the after-school commute. Tables 5.8 and 5.9 show the results of the regression analyses for models of school night crime and curfew hour crime, respectively. School night is defined as the period from 6 p.m. to 10 p.m. and the curfew period runs from 10 p.m. to 6 a.m. Both of these periods are generally unsupervised periods, in particular for older youth whose parents allow them to go out without supervision. Prince George's County has a nighttime curfew, so theoretically, the curfew period should be period that does not exhibit high rates of crime (assuming youth commit the majority of violent crimes). Results for these two periods are very similar. Table 5.8

Table 5.9. Instrumental Variables Regression with GHET of the Log of Violent Crime Rates on Place Risk, Guardianship, and Offender Presence, Curfew, 2000.

Variables	Curfew
Place Risk	
Presence of Youth Hangout	0.371**
Number of Busy Retail Places	0.401***
Guardianship-Routine Activity	
Pct. Owner-Occupied	−0.009***
Pct. One-Person Households	0.000
Pct. Renter Crowding	0.007
Bus Stop Count	—
Housing Density[†]	0.011**
Guardianship-Social Disorganization	
Pct. African Americans	0.006***
Racial Heterogeneity	0.154
Pct. Female Headed Households	0.002
Median Value Owner Housing[†]	−0.0004
Distance from City	−0.027***
Offender Presence	
Youth Arrests	0.012***
Control Variables	
Block Size	0.707***
Prior Victimization	0.029***
Zero Population	−0.797***
Spatial Lag	0.303***
Constant	−2.182***
East Side	2.336***
West Side	4.458***
R^2	0.27
Sq. Corr.	0.26
N	7,334.000

* $p<0.05$; **$p<0.01$; ***$p<0.001$.
[†]Coefficients for variable have been multiplied by 1,000.

(school night) shows that both place risk variables (youth hangouts and busy places) have a significant effect on violent crime. With regard to guardianship, the significant variables are owner occupied, housing density, percent African American, female-headed households, housing value, and distance from the District. Offender presence also has a strong influence on crime. Every ten additional arrests on a block results in a 20 percent increase in violent crime. Findings from the regression analyses on curfew time violent crime are similar to those during the school night. However, two social disorganization variables—female-headed households and housing values—are no longer significant in the model of school curfew crime. The number of youth arrests has twice the effect during the earlier time period then during the curfew time period. This finding coincides with the expectation that there

Table 5.10.   Instrumental Variables Regression with GHET of the Log of Violent Crime Rates on Place Risk, Guardianship, and Offender Presence, Weekend, 2000.

Variables	Weekend
Place Risk	
Presence of Youth Hangout	0.222
Number of Busy Retail Places	0.511***
Guardianship-Routine Activity	
Pct. Owner-Occupied	-0.008***
Pct. One-Person Households	-0.001
Pct. Renter Crowding	0.019
Bus Stop Count	—-
Housing Density[†]	0.006
Guardianship-Social Disorganization	
Pct. African Americans	0.005***
Racial Heterogeneity	0.394**
Pct. Female Headed Households	0.009**
Median Value Owner Housing[†]	-0.002***
Distance from City	-0.033***
Offender Presence	
Youth Arrests	0.019***
Control Variables	
Block Size	0.833***
Prior Victimization	0.026***
Zero Population	-1.356***
Spatial Lag	0.308***
Constant	-1.607***
East Side	3.726***
West Side	5.860***
R^2	0.25
Sq. Corr.	0.24
N	7,334.000

* $p<0.05$; **$p<0.01$; ***$p<0.001$.
[†]Coefficients for variable have been multiplied by 1,000.

will be fewer youth available as potential offenders or targets during the curfew period. The results of the remaining model in the first set of models (base model, no school characteristics) are shown in table 5.10. Not surprisingly, youth hangouts, as measured in this study, do not have a criminogenic effect during the weekend. Most of the youth hangouts are places where youth would congregate in larger concentrations after school as opposed to on weekends (e.g., recreation centers, private and parochial schools). Youth activity is more spread out during the weekends, as youth participate in any number of activities, including activities that bring them out of the study site. All social disorganization guardianship variables are associated with violent crime and offender presence is strongly associated with violent crime.

Results of Regression Models Examining Schools as Generators

The next group of models run is similar to the previous models, but includes three variables that represent school characteristics. These variables include block distance in miles to the closest school and two dummy variables that represent whether a block is close to a low-resource school ("resource deprivation") or a school whose average student characteristics have been linked to school disorder ("disorderly milieu"). Every block is assigned a school variable representing the name of the school that is the closest to the block. If a particular school scored a value of "1" for resource deprivation, all blocks that have been assigned that school receive the value of "1." The results of the regression analyses for these models are shown in tables 5.11 and 5.12. The number of busy retail places has a strong criminogenic effect during all time periods, but the effect is strongest during the evening, late at night, and in the summertime. Youth hangouts do not attract crime during the morning commute or on the weekends. The presence of a youth hangout has the greatest effect during the after-school period, supporting research hypothesis six. The effect of owner-occupancy is relatively stable over all time periods and bus stop count is highly significant in the models for which the variable is included. Renter housing and one-person households do not have a significant effect on crime in any of the time periods. Blocks that are racially heterogeneous are associated with violence during the school day, the weekend, and the summertime, with the largest effect during the weekend. It is not clear what these findings indicate. Housing density influences crime only at night; the coefficient is marginally significant (1.178E-05; p=.03).

Offender presence is associated with violent crime in all time periods, but has the largest effect during the nighttime. The control variables are significant during all time periods. The lower section of the tables contains the coefficients for the school variables. Distance to the closest school has a significant effect on violent crime only during the school day. Essentially, during the day schools are generators of crime.[1] An increase of one mile in the distance between a block and a school decreases violent crime rates by 4 percent. This finding is indicative of routine activity theory. Given that the majority of school age youth are in or near schools during the school day, it is highly likely that crime is higher in the blocks closest to the schools. Similarly, as youth disperse from school after school is over for the day, distance to school is less likely to matter, as the findings suggest. However, according to the findings (column 2 in table 5.11), blocks that are near schools that have high levels of resource deprivation have higher violent crime rates during the after-school period. On average, during the after-school period, blocks near low-resource schools have violent crime rates that are 10 percent higher than violent crime rates for blocks near high-resource schools. A relationship between school variables and violent crime was also

Table 5.11. Instrumental Variables Regression with GHET of the Log of Violent Crime Rates on Place Risk, Guardianship, Offender Presence, and School Characteristics by School Commute, School Session, and School Night, 2000.

Variables	AM Commute	PM Commute	School Session	School Night
Place Risk				
Presence of Youth Hangout	0.164	0.629**	0.505**	0.409*
Number of Retail Places	0.079***	0.349***	0.243***	0.389***
Guardianship-Routine Activity				
Pct. Owner-Occupied	−0.003**	−0.005***	−0.004***	−0.005***
Pct. One-Person Households	0.001	−0.001	−0.000	−0.002
Pct. Renter Crowding	0.007	0.009	−0.001	0.009
Bus Stop Count	0.012***	0.017***	—	—
Housing Density†	0.002	−0.000	−0.000	0.012*
Guardianship-Social Disorg.				
Pct. African Americans	0.002***	0.004***	0.003***	0.004***
Racial Heterogeneity	0.073	0.176	0.185*	0.171
Pct. Fem-Headed Hsholds.	0.002	0.008**	0.003	0.007**
Med. Value Housing†	−0.001*	−0.002***	−0.000	−0.001*
Distance from City	−0.014**	−0.025**	−0.011	−0.014
Offender Presence				
Youth Arrests	0.006***	0.019***	0.009***	0.022***
Control Variables				
Block Size	0.268***	0.468***	0.463***	0.626***
Prior Victimization	0.025***	0.025***	0.029***	0.025***
Zero Population	−0.268**	−0.665***	−.0320*	−0.742***
Spatial Lag	0.087	0.272***	0.140**	0.298***
School Variables				
Distance to Closest School	−0.011	−0.020	−0.035**	−0.002
Resource Deprivation	0.041	0.098*	0.040	−0.019
Disorderly Milieu	0.129**	0.043	0.042	0.095
Constant	−3.728***	−2.390***	−3.377***	−2.283***
East Side	1.135***	2.460***	1.625***	2.696***
West Side	2.501***	4.550***	3.003***	4.487***
R²	0.19	0.23	0.23	0.24
Sq. Corr.	0.19	0.23	0.22	0.24
N	7,334.000	7,334.000	7,334.000	7,334.000

* $p<0.05$; **$p<0.01$; ***$p<0.001$.
†Coefficients for variable have been multiplied by 1,000.

found for the morning school commute. Blocks near schools with a disorderly milieu (average characteristics of the student body) have a criminogenic effect. These areas experience violent crime rates that are 13 percent higher, on average than blocks that are not closest to disorderly milieu schools.

As hypothesized, none of the school variables influences violent crime during time periods *not* related to the routines of attending school (i.e., the weekend, school night, curfew, and summer). The spatial lag variable is significant in all models with the exception of the morning commute.

Table 5.12. Instrumental Variables Regression with GHET of the Log of Violent Crime Rates on Place Risk, Guardianship, Offender Presence, and School Characteristics by Curfew, Weekend, and Summer, 2000.

Variables	Curfew	Weekend	Summer
Place Risk			
Presence of Youth Hangout	0.371***	0.225	0.505**
Number of Busy Retail Places	0.401***	0.512***	0.481***
Guardianship-RA			
Pct. Owner-Occupied	−0.009***	−0.008***	−0.007***
Pct. One-Person Households	0.000	−0.001	−0.000
Pct. Renter Crowding	0.007	0.019	0.005
Bus Stop Count	—	—	—
Housing Density[†]	0.012*	0.006	0.005
Guardianship-Social Disorg.			
Pct. African Americans	0.005***	0.005***	0.006***
Racial Heterogeneity	0.181	0.421**	0.318**
Pct. Fem. Headed Households	0.002	0.009**	0.011***
Median Value Owner Housing[†]	−0.001	−0.000***	−0.000**
Distance from City	−0.029***	−0.037***	−0.020*
Offender Presence			
Youth Arrests	0.012***	0.019***	0.016***
Control Variables			
Block Size	0.704***	0.827***	0.906***
Prior Victimization	0.029***	0.026***	0.027***
Zero Population	−0.827***	−1.401***	−0.740***
Spatial Lag	0.281***	0.287***	0.310***
School Variables			
Distance to Closest School	0.003	0.013	−0.010
Resource	0.057	0.040	0.002
Disorderly Milieu	0.086	0.120	0.023
Constant	−2.251***	−1.661***	−2.155***
East Side	2.333***	3.723***	3.509***
West Side	4.456***	5.856***	5.286****
R^2	0.27	0.25	0.25
Sq. Corr.	0.26	0.25	0.24
N	7,334.000	7,334.000	7,334.000

* $p<0.05$; ** $p<0.01$; *** $p<0.001$.
[†]Coefficients for variable have been multiplied by 1,000.

Results of Regression Models Incorporating Interaction Effects

The final group of models run contains interactions between social disorganization variables and routine activity variables. As discussed earlier, the interaction terms between the following variables are tested: housing values and number of retail busy places; distance to school and retail busy places; distance to school and the presence of a youth hangout, housing density, and female-headed households; and female-headed households and youth arrests.

Table 5.13. Instrumental Variables Regression with GHET of the Log of Violent Crime Rates on Place Risk, Guardianship, and Offender Presence with Interaction Terms, by Time of Day, 2000.

Variables	AM Commute	PM Commute	School Session	School Night
Place Risk				
Presence of Youth Hangout	0.342	0.423	−0.036	0.262
Number of Busy Places	−0.007	0.273***	0.324***	0.247***
Guardianship-RA				
Pct. Owner-Occupied	−0.005**	−0.004***	−0.004***	−0.005***
Pct. One-Person Households	0.001	−0.000	−0.000	−0.002
Pct. Renter Crowding	0.006	0.009	−0.001	0.009
Bus Stop Count	0.007***	0.016***	—	—
Housing Density[†]	−0.019**	−0.044***	−0.042***	−0.034***
Guardianship-Social Dis.				
Pct. African Americans	0.002***	0.004***	0.002***	0.004***
Racial Heterogeneity	0.079	0.162	0.190**	0.160
Pct. Fem-Headed Hholds.	−0.001	0.005	−0.001	0.004
Med Value Housing[†]	−0.001*	−0.001**	−0.000	−0.001*
Distance from City	−0.013*	−0.237**	−0.012*	−0.012
Offender Presence				
Youth Arrests	0.016***	0.054***	0.029***	0.057***
Control Variables				
Block Size	0.230***	0.379***	0.416***	0.514***
Prior Victimization	0.026***	0.028***	0.031***	0.029***
Zero Population	−0.261*	−0.651***	−0.333*	−0.727***
Spatial Lag	0.113***	0.271***	0.118***	0.292***
School Variables				
Distance to Closest School	−0.013	−0.023	−0.336**	−0.009
Resource Deprivation	0.034	0.084	0.037	−0.035
Disorderly Milieu	0.122**	0.331	0.036	0.090
Interactions				
Hous. Value*Retail Busy[†]	−0.000	−0.001**	−0.001***	−0.001**
Busy Places*Dist. School	0.086**	0.148***	0.015	0.232***
Hangout*Dist. School	−0.109	0.216	0.456***	0.207
House Dens*Fem-Headed[†]	0.002***	0.003***	0.003***	0.004***
Yth Arrests*Fem-Headed	−0.001***	−0.002***	−0.001***	−0.002***
Constant	−3.673***	−2.430***	−3.467	−2.444***
East Side	1.127***	2.415***	1.598***	2.649***
West Side	2.493***	4.493***	2.676***	4.412***
Multicollinearity Cond. No.	24.9	24.9	24.9	24.9
R²	.19	.24	.23	.25
Sq. Corr.	.19	.24	.23	.25
N	7,334.000	7,334.000	7,334.000	7,334.000

Table 5.13. *(continued)*

Variables	Curfew	Weekend	Summer
Place Risk			
Presence of Youth Hangout	0.015	−0.144	−0.089
Number of Busy Retail Places	0.268***	0.361***	0.332***
Guardianship- Routine Activity			
Pct. Owner-Occupied	−0.008***	−0.000***	−0.006***
Pct. One-Person Households	0.001	−0.001	0.0002
Pct. Renter Crowding	0.008	0.019*	0.005
Bus Stop Count	—	—	—
Housing Density[†]	−0.033***	−0.048***	−0.043***
Guardianship-Social Disorg.			
Pct. African Americans	0.005***	0.004***	0.006***
Racial Heterogeneity	0.185	0.411***	0.313**
Pct. Female Headed Households	−0.002	0.0042	0.007*
Median Value Owner Housing[†]	−0.000	−0.002***	−0.001*
Distance from City	−0.027**	−0.036***	−0.175*
Offender Presence			
Youth Arrests	0.041***	0.059***	0.051***
Control Variables			
Block Size	0.590***	0.691***	0.766***
Prior Victimization	0.031***	0.029***	0.030***
Zero Population	−0.815***	−1.383***	−0.727***
Spatial Lag	0.271***	0.263***	0.307***
School Variables			
Distance to Closest School	−0.005	0.004	−0.021
Resource Deprivation	0.047	0.234	−0.011
Disorderly Milieu	0.088	0.123*	0.020
Interactions			
Housing Value*Retail Busy[†]	−0.001**	−0.001**	−0.001***
Busy Places*Dist. School	0.267***	0.287***	0.301***
Hangout*Dist. School	0.393**	0.426*	0.650***
Housing Dens*Fem-Headed[†]	0.004***	0.004***	0.004***
Youth Arrests*Fem-Headed	−0.001***	−0.002***	−0.000***
Constant	−2.327***	−1.776***	−2.213***
East Side	2.258***	3.609***	3.445
West Side	4.399***	5.771***	5.190
Multicollinearity Cond. No.	24.9	24.9	24.9
R^2	.28	.26	.26
Sq. Corr.	.28	.26	.26
N	7,334.000	7,334.000	7,334.000

* $p<0.05$; ** $p<0.01$; *** $p<0.001$.
[†]Coefficients for variable have been multiplied by 1,000.

Table 5.13 shows the regression results. Retail busy places are not at equal risk of violent crime across all blocks. Retail busy places are less likely to attract crime in blocks characterized by higher socioeconomic status (as measured by housing values). Not surprisingly, this relationship is significant during all time periods except the morning school commute period.

Looking at the interactions involving distance to school, the direction of the observed effects for these interactions are not in the expected direction. During all time periods, except the school session/day, blocks with retail busy places have higher violent crime rates as distance from a school increases. In other words, schools do not add additional opportunity for crime to nearby blocks with a larger number of retail busy places. However, it is interesting that the interaction effect is not significant during the time period when youth are in school and, hence, occupied.

The effect of the interaction between distance to school and the presence of a youth hangout is also not in the expected direction. For blocks with youth hangouts, every additional mile the block is from a school increases the violent crime rate 8 percent (sum of .456\-.342\-.336) during the school day. When the interaction terms are added to the school day crime model, the main effect of the presence of a youth hangout disappears (and the coefficient is negative). The same processes are at work during the curfew period, the weekend, and the summertime. These findings run counter to the hypotheses that state that the degree to which schools act as generators would be magnified in the presence of other land uses that provide opportunity for violence. The main effect of distance to school remains significant in the school day model and increases tenfold from the effect achieved when interactions are not included in the model.

The product terms of housing density and percent of households that are female-headed are significant and in the expected direction in all models. In blocks with high housing density, the effect of high percentages of female-headed households on violence is intensified, supporting the hypothesis that physical features of the environment (density) interact with neighborhood structural constraints that reduce social guardianship (as measured by percentage of households headed by women). The relationship holds across all time periods. There is a reduction in the main effect of percent female-headed households, and the main effect of housing density becomes negative. Essentially, it is within the context of large percentages of female-headed households that high housing density increases violence. High housing density not coupled with female-headed households is associated with decreases in the rate of violence. This may be that more crowded areas actually deter violence (more housing equates to more people which provided more guardianship) but high-density areas comprised of female-headed households reduces guardianship in that there are more youth and less adults. Another interesting finding is associated with interactions involving the percentage of households that are headed by females. The interaction between youth arrests and female-headed households has a negative effect, although a very small effect, on crime. The main effects of youth arrests and female-headed households remain positive. Examining the coefficients in the full model indicates that including the interaction barely changes the relationship (sum of .007\.051\-.000; summertime model). A discussion of this finding, as well as all findings from all regression models, is provided in the next and final chapter.

Unique Variance Explained by Variable Clusters

To examine the relative importance of the variable clusters, commonality analysis was performed. When independent variables are uncorrelated, a simple index of the importance of the variables is the zero order correlations of each independent variable and the dependent variable (Cohen and Cohen 1983). With regard to the independent variables used in this study, the variables are correlated, and hence, one cannot examine the zero order correlations. Instead, this analysis tests the increment in R^2 as variables are added to the equation. Proc GLM in SAS was used to obtain the Type III sum of squares for each independent variable. The estimates of coefficients and error terms derived from the SAS GLM models were very similar to the instrumental variables spatial lag model results of SpaceStat. SAS was used because SpaceStat does not automatically compute the Type III sums of squares for each variable. In addition, the psuedo R^2 obtained in SpaceStat is not appropriate for deriving unique variances. With regard to the Proc GLM output, the Type III sums of squares can be divided by the total sum of squares to derive the proportion of variance in the dependent variable uniquely attributed to each independent variable.

Table 5.14 shows the unique variance explained with regard to the violent crime rate for each variable in the school session model (interactions not included), as well as the total unique variance explained for each cluster of variables. The unique variance explained is less than one percent for all variable clusters with the exception of the routine activity variables (1.8 percent). The routine activity variables are more strongly associated with violent crime than are the social disorganization variables. The school-related place risk variables have less of an impact on violent crime than the other clusters of variables. Only 2 percent (1.79 + 0.11 + 0.09 + 0.04) of the variance can be uniquely attributable to one or the other of the four sets of variables, out of a total of 23 percent. This implies that much of the remaining

Table 5.14.   Unique Variance Explained (Pct.).

Variable Cluster	School Session Model
Place Risk/Routine Activity Variables	*Variance Explained*
Presence of Youth Hangout	0.06%
Number of Busy Retail Places	1.11
Pct. Owner-Occupied	0.23
Pct. One-Person Households	0.00
Pct. Renter Crowding	0.00
Bus Stop Count	0.45
Housing Density	0.00
Total-Routine Activity	1.79%
Social Disorganization	
Pct. African Americans	0.01%
Racial Heterogeneity	0.02
Pct. Female Headed Households	0.01
Median Value Owner Housing	0.01
Distance from City	0.06
Total-Social Disorganization	0.11%
Offender Presence	
Youth Arrests	0.09%
Total-Offender Presence	0.09%
School Place Risk	
Distance to Closest School	0.03%
Resource Deprivation	0.004
Disorderly Milieu	0.001
Total-School Place Risk	0.04%
Control Variables	
Block Size	0.35%
Prior Victimization	3.60
Zero Population	0.07
Spatial Lag	0.01
Total R^2	0.23
N	7,334.000

variance (20 percent) is shared by the blocks of variables and/or can be attributed to the control variables and spatial lag (4 percent is uniquely attributable to the control variables (block size, prior victimization).

NOTE

1. This statement is not meant to suggest causality. Basically, schools act as opportunity magnets.

Chapter Six

Discussion and Conclusion

This study is designed to elaborate understanding of the role of schools in generating block-level violence rates. The study examines schools, using opportunity theories and social disorganization theory to identify attributes of blocks and other crime generators found on blocks, such as youth hangouts and food and retail establishments, that provide the opportunity for crime. The study introduces distance from schools to blocks to provide a more precise measure of the opportunity afforded by crime generators and adds time of day and week to further refine the assessment of the effects of crime generators. The effects of the ebb and flow of youth from schools past blocks will vary in time and distance from schools. This variability permits the assessment of the effects of crime generators more precisely than in previous work. The study hypothesizes that violent crime will be inversely related to distance from school and occur only during time periods associated with the presence of large numbers of youth.

Routine activity theory posits that large urban schools act as magnets for youth. As the number of youth present increases, so too does the opportunity for violence. Essentially, more youth equals more targets and more opportunity to turn potential offenders into *actual* offenders. Routine activity theory also suggests that certain school environments or settings will generate more opportunity for violence than other settings. Schools that are low on resources will be more likely to have less adequate supervision of youth, providing more opportunity for crime. Schools with reduced capacity to supervise or guard students from potential offenders create additional opportunities for offending.

Variables representing three main constructs derived from routine activity theory, defensible space theory and social disorganization theory are used to evaluate models predicting violent crime rates. The variables representing these constructs, physical place risk, guardianship, and potential offenders, are hypothesized to explain variations in violence depending on the daily routines of youth. If the hypothesized patterns are not observed, one must question the effects of attractors in generating violence. In addition, the study permits the disaggregation of crime opportunity effects into the appropriate opportunity theory, that is, routine activity or social disorganization, at the same time exploring theoretical integration.

The findings provide support for the relationship between physical place risk, guardianship and the presence of motivated offenders. The first set of models indicate that almost all variables examined are related to violence at the block level. However, some of the guardianship variables (housing density, renter crowding, and housing value) do not have an effect on violence during times of the day when youth are in school or on their way to and from school. In general, renter crowding and percentage of one-person households are not good predictors of violent crime. It may be that one-person households do not adequately measure the provision of guardianship. These households may not be working households (could possible be retired older individuals), and therefore the individuals would be more likely to provide some capacity for place guardianship. Overall, the findings regarding the neighborhood context variables (i.e., the social disorganization variables) indicate that the flow of youth away from their homes to school overshadows the effects of neighborhood social organizational context on violence. Female-headed households and housing values do not influence crime during the school day but have a significant impact on violence rates after youth leave school for the day. Similarly, the effect of racial heterogeneity on violent crime is very small and generally stable (and in some models nonsignificant) Monday through Friday, but the effect doubles during the weekend. Another social disorganization variable exhibits the largest effect during the weekend—distance from central city. These findings suggest that weekend routine activities may bring about very different types of opportunity for violent crime. With regard to racial heterogeneity, future research examining neighborhood effects on crime can benefit by incorporating a time dimension or by examining in more detail the processes that bring victims and offenders together.

The second set of research hypotheses assert that schools—the simple *presence* of schools—act as generators of crime during the times of day associated with youth attending school. The findings suggest that the presence of schools, as measured by distance between a block and a school, are generators of crime during the period of time when youth are in school: 10 a.m. through 2 p.m., Mondays through Fridays. Distance to school did not have an effect on crime during the after-school period. This lack of significance in the after-school period suggests that there may be no great concentration of youth nearby schools between 2 p.m. and 6 p.m. Youth are more likely to disperse from schools quickly, moving to their next destination. As the findings indicate, their next destination is likely to be a place such as a mall or recreation center—somewhere to hang out with friends after school. It is possible that the models would have shown an effect in the after-school period if the models examined a reduced after-school period to represent the hours immediately after school—such as 2 p.m. to 4 p.m. Regardless, the findings support routine activity theory.

When school characteristics are included in the models, the findings suggest that schools that lack order and schools characterized by resource deprivation are generators of violence during the school commuting period. More specifically, resource-deprived schools exhibit an influence on violence after school, and schools whose student population, on average, has characteristics associated with school disorder and crime, influence violence during the morning commute. The findings suggest that as youth disperse from resource-deprived schools, they may do so in a disorderly fashion, and this disorder spills over into the communities in which those schools are situated (resource deprivation would lead to low supervision and more likelihood of disorderly after-school period). An alternative hypothesis is that because low resource schools are often situated in low resource communities, the resource deprivation variable is simply capturing a neighborhood effect not measured by other variables in the model. It is not clear why the two school characteristic variables—resource deprivation and disorderly milieu—exhibit effects in different time periods. It may be that differences in timing of the effects are related to the differences that are associated with how youth flow into schools in the morning and exit schools in the afternoon. In the morning, youth are more concentrated into the areas where schools are situated, since the majority of all middle school— and high school–aged youth are flowing, roughly at the same time, into the forty-five schools in the study site. During the after-school period, youth are exiting at different times and to many hundreds of different places. In the morning, school characterized by a disorderly milieu may have less control over the large number of youth that need adequate supervision, therefore, the characteristics of the students themselves may play a part in creating sufficient opportunity for violent crime to occur. During the after-school period, there will be lower concentrations of these youth as youth disperse to different places and at different times. However, regardless of the disorderly milieu, schools deprived of resources may not be able to adequately supervise students as they are released into the community. Future research could examine additional characteristics of schools to assist in determining the different processes operating during the morning school commute and after-school period.

The findings from the models that incorporate interaction effects provide only limited support for hypotheses that some routine activity variables are conditional on neighborhood structural constraints. Two of the three interactions that examined the product of a routine activity variable and a social disorganization variable were significant in the expected direction. Areas characterized by higher housing values diminish the strong effect that retail busy places have on violence. The density of housing influences violent crime rates in those areas with high percentages of female-headed households. The main effect of housing density becomes negative, signifying that the effects of housing density on crime may be the result of complex interaction of a number of land use and neighborhood structural variables. Research on violent places could benefit from studies examining housing density in more detail. Also of interest is the finding that the positive relationship found between violence and the number of youth arrests is conditioned by female-headed households. Female-headed households exhibit a negative impact on the relationship. Blocks with high percentages of female-headed households and large numbers of youth arrests have a somewhat lower rate of violence. It appears that arrests may be somewhat of a deterrent in areas generally associated with lower socioeconomic status. Perhaps the youth arrested in these areas are being detained longer or have been incarcerated. This finding is consistent with the literature establishing a negative relationship between arrest and crime.

The literature examining places has focused on interactions effects in hope of advancing theoretical integration of routine activity theory and social disorganization theory. The results of this study partially support this integration. Previous research that did not find support for integration may have used a level of geography, such as the block group or census tract, which was too large to provide sufficient variation to examine context. Spatial heterogeneity can cause problems in studies using large areas. For example, heterogeneity may exist in a residential census tract where the tract is actually comprised of one block group that is residential and one block group that is a park. The tract would be classified as residential, ignoring the differential opportunity afforded by parkland. Others have used the now classic example of a tract that is classified as racially heterogeneous when in fact residents of one side of the tract are all African American and residents of the other part of the tract are white (Smith, Frazee, and Davison 2000). The future of research on places could be advanced by examination of interaction effects, whether using a multilevel approach or the approach used in this study. This problem of within-unit heterogeneity can result in attenuation of effects and further confound interpretations of model variables.

The results of this study are limited by the data available. The study examined violent crime rates in a domain specific model relating to the daily routines of youth, using violent victimizations reported to the police as the dependent variable. The study makes the assumption that much of the violence committed is committed by youth. This assumption cannot be examined explicitly given the data at hand. Information about the offender is not known in this study. The dependent variable includes victimizations of all ages. Limiting the victimizations to include only youth victims would limit the study to only explaining crime against youth. Past research indicates that youth are committing crimes against individuals in their age group, as well as individuals not in their age group (Gouvis, Johnson and Roth 1997; Gouvis et al. 1999). In addition, the data are limited in that crime is likely to be underreported, given the reliance on crime reported to the police. Crime may be more underreported near schools.

With regard to understanding the crime-generating characteristics of schools, this study is somewhat limited in that aggregate data on individual schools, beyond what was used for this study, are difficult to collect. The school variables were used to develop two constructs representing school climate. The school system in the study site was resistant to outside research at a time when the school district was in great flux with the start of a new school administrator, budget cuts, and new busing practices. New busing practices do not affect the study or data collected. Data were collected through 2001. New busing practices did not begin until the fall of 2002. Future studies could include additional variables that characterize specific management practices of schools (e.g., the extent of disciplinary actions, class room sizes, etc.) or that aggregate survey data from students on school attitudes and atmosphere. With additional school-level data, methods such as two- or three-level modeling could be used to examine with more precision variations in rates of violence. The current study relies on dummy variables to indicate whether a block is near a low resource or disorderly milieu school.

The limited development of software to analyze spatial econometric models of a phenomenon such as crime, which exhibits nonnormal distributions across small geographic areas, confines the opportunity to explore alternative models to analyze the data in this study. Instrumental variables regression models incorporating spatial lag in the presence of a large number of blocks with no crimes may lead to inefficient coefficient estimates. Hence, the models used in this study may underestimate significant effects. Software tools to handle this type of problem are currently in development (Anselin 2002).

IMPLICATIONS OF CURRENT STUDY

The research findings suggest that adequate supervision of youth during vulnerable *times* and in vulnerable *places* is critical to public safety. Understanding how *time* intersects with other variables has implications for policing and community problem solving. The ebb and flow of youth going about their daily routines coincides with levels of violence. Individuals are vulnerable to violence during times when the flow of youth is highly concentrated. At certain times of day there will be *places* with high concentrations of youth, and limited adult supervision. Areas where large numbers of youth come together to wait for the school bus are particularly vulnerable, as evidenced by findings demonstrating that violence rates increase roughly 7 percent with every ten youth congregating at bus stops. More specifically, in the after-school period, crowded bus stops generate even more crime—an additional ten youth raise violence rates almost 20 percent.

In addition to bus stops, there are other *places* where youth patronize as part of their daily activities—places such as malls and movie theaters and recreation centers—are risky places after school and into the late-night period on school nights. The findings indicate that although it is likely for youth to patronize these places during weekends, it is the times of day that are most likely to witness the greatest concentration of youth that experience the highest rates of violence. Rates of violence were highest in the after-school period in places that have youth hangouts. As the afternoon passes into the evening and late night, rates of violence decrease in blocks that have youth hangouts. Supervision, whether it is increased police surveillance, parental oversight, or other adults acting as capable guardians (e.g., recreation center staff, security at malls) may be important in limiting opportunities for violence.

It seems obvious that a study examining vulnerable time periods will conclude that increased police supervision during high crime times is warranted. The findings of this study warrant more than simply increased police presence as youth leave school. The findings suggest that policing practice could benefit by following the flow of youth across different time periods of the day and week in conjunction with recognition that certain school climates may impact violence far into the communities as youth leave school and disperse to their next activities.

Furthermore, the implications of this study go beyond simply addressing schools as generators of crime. Techniques and statistical models used in this study can be applied to studies examining placement of other institutions and establishments such as halfway houses, community and recreation centers, or police substations. The field is open for studies examining characteristics of establishments that act as crime attractors and generators, or crime buffers. Police crime analysts currently using advanced techniques for hotspot mapping could benefit by going beyond hotspot analyses to incorporate aggregate data models on small areas. The data used in this study are often readily available to police in large urban jurisdictions. Even without the use of advanced methods, time of day should factor into the analytical techniques used by police departments and researchers examining crime in small places.

With regard to specific times, police supervision is needed in blocks near schools during the school day (10 a.m. to 2 p.m.), as evidenced by findings that a block's distance from a school has a significant impact on violence during the time when it is assumed that youth are in the classroom. Given the probability that crime on or near school campuses will be underreported (i.e., crime may be reported to school authorities and not to the police) the finding that distance to school matters during the school day is striking. School policies on truancy (skipping classes or arriving late and leaving early) and lunchtime schedules and activities should be re-examined.

School settings must also be examined more closely to determine additional methods to diminish opportunities for offending. The study suggests that schools that lack resources could be contributing to opportunities for violence by not providing adequate supervision after school. Past research on school disorder concurs with these findings. Schools that are successful in general management functions, such as resource allocation, experience less crime (Gottfredson and Gottfredson 1985; Gottfredson, Wilson, and Najaka 2002). These well-managed schools create environments in which school staff interact with students, and in turn, boost informal social control.

If schools are influencing rates of crime, schools can have a larger role in preventing crime not only in the immediate vicinity of schools, but also farther away from schools into the community. Recent research evaluating school crime prevention and intervention programs shows hope for programs that aim to bolster pro-social norms and integrate a strong sense of social organization into school life (Gottfredson, Wilson, and Najaka, 2002). Given the current study's findings that disorderly milieus and resource deprivation of schools may be related to community violence, school prevention, and intervention programs that are effective in reducing violence in schools could have great potential for reducing community crime during the school commute period and in the early evenings. The modest federal spending on crime prevention in schools should be re-evaluated, particularly in light of findings indicating that school-based prevention is more cost effective than other programs such as child home visits, parent training, and intensive supervision of justice system-involved youth (Greenwood et al. 1996).

With regard to research, studies examining violence in places should continue to examine interaction effects in hope of uncovering further insight into how opportunity is created by different land use characteristics in conjunction with neighborhood factors such as poverty. The finding that high housing density (housing per square mile) provides more opportunity for violence in neighborhoods characterized by larger percentages of female-headed households, but the main effect of housing density becomes negative, has implications for policymakers and local government officials with regard to zoning, housing construction, and land use development. Furthermore, understanding these neighborhood processes will assist research seeking to understand the dynamics of neighborhood informal social control. As sociologists and community practitioners continue efforts to uncover methods to inform the development of neighborhood social control, research examining the micro-level conditions of neighborhoods that support and deter violence will be essential.

In addition, it is critical that criminal justice research re-examine what is known about variations in crime risk across time periods. For the last five years, reports of crime statistics on vulnerable times for youth rely solely on a few studies emphasizing 3 p.m. as the peak time for violent victimization involving juveniles (Richters, 1993; Sickmund, Snyder, and Poe-Yamagata 1997; Snyder and Sickmund 1995; Snyder 1999). The reliance on a limited number of studies is shortsighted and encumbering. Research and practice can only benefit by continuing to explore the myriad of factors that interface with time of day, week, year and season, to influence opportunity for violent crime.

CONCLUSION

In the introduction to *Violence in American Schools*, the authors state, "over the past decade there has been an epidemic of youth crime. The violence on the streets and in some of our homes has spilled over into the schools" (Elliott, Hamburg, and Williams 1998, 3). Perhaps it is time to expand our perspective to include the possibility that violence from schools is spilling over into the community. Although the current study does not directly address how violence manifests itself and spreads over time, the findings indicate that certain school climates may create crime opportunity not only in the vicinity of schools, but throughout communities as well. Offenders commit crime in areas where their routine activities take them. The routine activities of youth take them to and from school, in the path of many settings along the way.

Works Cited

Alexander, Rand Curtis, C. M. 1995. "A Critical Review of Strategies to Reduce School Violence." *Social Work in Education* 17(2):73–82.

Anderson, C. S. 1982. "A Search for School Climate: A Review of the Literature." *Review of Educational Research* 52:368–420.

Anderson, David, Sylvia Chenery, and Ken Pease. 1995. *Preventing Repeat Victimizations: A Report on Progress on Huddersfield.* Home Office Police Research Group Briefing Note 4/95. London: Home Office.

Anselin, L. 1984. "Specification Tests and Model Selection for Aggregate Spatial interaction, an Empirical Comparison." *Journal of Regional Science* 24:1–15.

———. 1988a. *Spatial Econometrics: Methods and Models.* Dordrecht: Kluwer Academic.

———. 1988b. "LaGrange Multiplier Test Diagnostics for Spatial Dependence and Spatial Heterogeneity." *Geographical analysis* 20:1–17.

———. 1989. *What Is Special about Spatial Data.* Technical Report 89-4. Santa Barbara: University of California, Santa Barbara, National Center for Geographic information and analysis. (Contained on CD-ROM. Fundamental research in geographic information and analysis. Santa Barbara: National Center for Geographic information and analysis.)

———. 1992. *SpaceStat Tutorial. A Workbook for Using SpaceStat in the Analysis of Spatial Data.* Urbana–Champaign: University of Illinois.

———. 2002. Personal communication between Luc Anselin and author via e-mail, October 15.

Astor, R. A., H. A. Meyer, and W. J. Behre. 1999. "Unowned Places and Times: Maps and interviews about Violence in High Schools." *American Educational Research Journal* 36(1):3–42.

Balkin, S. 1979. "Victimization Rates, Safety and Fear of Crime." *Social Problems* 26:343–58.

Barclay, P., J. Buchley, P. J. Brantingham, P. Brantingham, and T. Whinn-Yates. 1996. "Preventing Auto Theft in Suburban Vancouver Commuter Lots: Effects of a Bike

Patrol." In *Preventing Mass Transit Crime. Crime Prevention Studies, Volume. 6*, ed. R. V. Clarke. Monsey, NY: Criminal Justice Press.

Barker, R. G. 1968. *Ecological Psychology*. Stanford: University of California Press.

Barker, R. G., T. Dembo, and K. Lewin. 1943. "Frustration and Regression." In *Child Behavior and Development*, ed. R. G. Barker, J. S. Kounin, and H. F. Wright. New York: McGraw-Hill.

Barr, R., and K. Pease, 1990. "Crime Placement, Displacement, and Deflection." In *Crime and Justice: A Review of Research, Volume 12*, ed. M. Tonry and N. Morris. Chicago: University of Chicago Press.

Bastion, L. 1993. *Criminal Victimization, 1992*. Washington, DC: Bureau of Justice Statistics.

Baum A., J. E. Singer, and S. Valins, eds. 1978. *Advances in Environmental Psychology: Volume 1: The Urban Environment*. New York: John Wiley and Sons.

Beavon, D. J., J. K. Beavon, P. L. Brantingham, and P. J. Brantingham. 1994. "The Influence of Street Networks on the Patterning of Property Offenses." In *Crime Prevention Studies 2*, ed. R. V. Clark, 115–48. New York: Criminal Justice Press.

Belsley, D., E. Kuh, and R. Welsch. 1980. *Regression Diagnostics, Identifying Influential Data and Sources of Multicollinearity*. New York: Wiley.

Birkbeck, C., and G. LaFree. 1993. "The Situational Analysis of Crime and Deviance." *Annual Review of Sociology* 19:113–37.

Block, R., and C. R. Block. 2000. "The Bronx and Chicago: Street Robbery in the Environs of Rapid Transit Stations." In *Analyzing Crime Patterns: Frontiers of Practice*, ed. V. Goldsmith, P. G. McGuire, J. H. Mollenkopf and T. A. Ross. Thousand Oaks, CA: Sage Publications.

Blumstein, A., J. Cohen, and D. Nagin. 1978. *Deterrence and incapacitation: Estimating the Effects of Criminal Sanctions on Crime Rates*. Washington, DC: National Academy of Sciences.

Blumstein, A., J. Cohen, and R. Rosenfeld. 1991. "Trend and Deviation in Crime Rates: A Comparison of UCR and NCVS Data for Burglary and Robbery." *Criminology* 29:237–248.

Bordua, D. J. 1958. "Juvenile Delinquency and Anomie: An Attempt at Replication." *Social Problems* 6:230–38.

Brantingham, P., D. A. Dyreson, and P. Brantingham. 1976. "Crime Seen through A Cone of Resolution." *American Behavioral Scientist* (November–December).

Brantingham, P. J., and P. L. Brantingham. 1978. "A Theoretical Model of Crime Site Selection." In *Crime, Law, and Sanctions: Theoretical Perspectives*, ed. R. L. Akers and M. D. Krohn. Beverly Hills: Sage Publications.

———. 1982. "Mobility, Notoriety and Crime: A Study in Crime Patterns of Urban Nodal Points." *Journal of Environmental Systems* 11:89–99.

———. 1991. Introduction. In *Environmental Criminology*, 2nd edition, ed. P. J. Brantingham and P. L. Brantingham. Prospect Heights, IL: Waveland Press.

Brantingham, P. L., and P. J. Brantingham. 1994. "Crime Analysis Using Location Quotients." In *Proceedings of the International Seminar on Environmental Criminology and Crime Analysis*, ed. D. Zahm and P. Cromwell. Tallahassee: Florida Statistical Analysis Center, Florida Criminal Justice Institute.

———. 1995. "Criminality of Place: Crime Generators and Crime Attractors." *European Journal of Criminal Policy and Research* 3:5–26.

Breusch, T., and A. Pagan. 1979. "A Simple Test for Heteroskedasticity and Random Coefficient Variation." *Econometrica* 47:1287–94.

Bryk, A., and D. Driscoll. 1988. *The High School as Community: Contextual Influences and Consequences for Students and Teachers.* Madison: Center for Educational Research, University of Wisconsin.

Burgess, E. W. 1925. "The Growth of the City." In *The City*, ed. R. E. Park, E. W. Burgess, R. D. Mckenzie, and L. Wirth. Chicago: University of Chicago Press.

Bursik, R. J. 1999. "The Informal Control of Crime through Neighborhood Networks." *Sociological Focus* 32:85–97.

Bursik, R. J., and H. G. Grasmick. 1993. *Neighborhoods and Crime: The Dimensions of Effective Community Control.* New York: Lexington Books.

Cameron, A. C., and P. K. Trivedi. 1998. *Regression Analysis of Count Data.* Cambridge: Cambridge University Press.

Chilton, R. J. 1964. "Community in Delinquency Area Research: A Comparison of Studies for Baltimore, Detroit, and Indianapolis." *American Sociological Review* 28:826–34.

Clarke, R. V. 1980. "Situational Crime Prevention: Theory and Practice." *British Journal of Criminology* 20:136–147.

———. 1984. "Opportunity Based Crime Rates: The Difficulty of Further Refinement." *British Journal of Criminology* 24:74–83.

———, ed. 1992. *Situational Crime Prevention: Successful Case Studies.* Albany, NY: Harrow and Heston.

Clarke, R. V., and D. B. Cornish. 1985. "Modeling Offenders' Decisions: A Framework for Policy and Research." In *Crime and Justice: An Annual Review of Research, Volume 6*, ed. M. Tonry and N. Morris. Chicago: University of Chicago Press.

Clarke, R. V,. and M. Felson. 1993. *Routine Activity and Rational Choice. Advances in Criminological theory, Volume 5.* New Brunswick, NJ: Transaction Publishers.

Cohen, J., and P. Cohen. 1983. *Applied Regression/Correlation Analysis for Behavioral Science.* Hilldale, NJ: Lawrence Erlbaum.

Cohen, L., and D. Cantor. 1981. "Residential Burglary in the United States: Lifestyle and Demographic Factors Associated with the Probability of Victimization." *Journal of Research in Crime and Delinquency* 18:113–27.

Cohen, L., and M. Felson. 1979. "Social Change and Crime Rate Trends: A Routine Activity Approach." *American Sociological Review* 44:588–608.

Cohen, L. E., and D. Cantor. 1980. "The Determinants of Larceny: An Empirical and Theoretical Study." *Journal of Research in Crime and Delinquency* 17:140–59.

Cohen, L. E., J. R. Kluegel, and K. C. Land. 1981. "Social Inequality and Predatory Criminal Victimization: An Exposition and Test of a Formal Theory." *American Sociological Review* 46:505–24.

Cook, P. J. 1985. "The Demand and Supply of Criminal Opportunities." Working Paper, Durham, NC: Institute of Policy Sciences and Public Affairs, Duke University.

Davidson, R. N. 1989. "Micro-Environments of Violence." In *The Geography of Crime*, ed. David J. Evans and David T. Herbert, 59–85. New York: Routledge.

Duke, D. L. 1989. "School Organization, Leadership, and Student Behavior." In *Strategies to Reduce Student Misbehavior*, ed. Oliver C. Moles. Washington, DC: Office of Educational Research and Improvement.

Dunteman, G. H. 1989. *Principal Components Analysis*. Sage University Paper Series. Quantitative Applications in the Social Sciences. Newbury Park, CA.

Eck, J. E. 1994. "Drug Markets and Drug Places: A Case-Control Study of the Spatial Structure of Illicit Drug Dealing." Ph.D. dissertation. University of Maryland, College Park.

———. 1997. "Preventing Crime at Places." In *Preventing Crime: What Works, What Doesn't, What's Promising. A Report to the United States Congress*, ed. L. W. Sherman, D. Gottfredson, D. Mackenzie, J. E. Eck, P. Reuter, and S. Bushway. College Park: University of Maryland Press.

Eck, J. E., and D. Weisburd. 1995. *Crime and Place*. Monsey, NY: Criminal Justice Press and Police Executive Research Forum.

Elliott, D. S., B. Hamburg, and K. R. Williams. 1998. *Violence in American Schools: A New Perspective*. Cambridge: Cambridge University Press.

Fagan, J., and G. Davies. 2000. "Crime in Public Housing: Two-Way Diffusion Effects in Surrounding Neighborhoods." In *Analyzing Crime Patterns: Frontiers of Practice*, ed. V. Goldsmith, P. G. Mcguire, J. H. Mollenkopf, and T. A. Ross. Thousand Oaks, CA: Sage Publications.

Federal Register. 1999. Part 3. Department of Justice, Office of Juvenile Justice and Delinquency Prevention. Field-initiated Research and Evaluation. Federal Register, vol. 64, no. 143. Program Notice. Tuesday, July 27.

Felson, M. 1986. "Routine Activities, Social Controls, Rational Decisions and Criminal Outcomes." In *The Reasoning Criminal*, ed. D. Cornish and R. V. Clarke. New York: Springer-Verlag.

———. 1987. "Routine Activities and Crime Prevention in the Developing Metropolis." *Criminology* 25(4):911–31.

———. 1994. *Crime and Everyday Life: Insight and Implications for Society*. Thousand Oaks, CA: Pine Forge Press.

———. 1995. "Those Who Discourage Crime." In *Crime and Place, Volume 4*, ed. J. E. Eck and D. Weisburd, 53–66. Monsey, NY: Criminal Justice Press.

Felson, M., and L. Cohen. 1980. "Human Ecology and Crime: A Routine Activity Approach." *Human Ecology* 8:389–406.

Felson, M., and M. Gottfredson. 1984. "Adolescent Activities Near Peers and Parents." *Journal of Marriage and the Family* 46:709–14.

Felson, R. B. 1997. "Routine Activities and Involvement in Violence as Actor, Witness, or Target." *Violence and Victims* 12(3):209–21.

Fisher, B., and J. L. Nasar. 1992." Fear of Crime in Relation to Three Exterior Site Features: Prospect, Refuge and Escape". *Environment and Behavior* 24:35–65.

Gabor, T. 1990. "Crime Displacement and Situational Prevention: Toward the Development of Some Principles." *Canadian Journal of Criminology* 32:41–74.

Gaquin, D. A., and M. S. Littman, ed. 1999. *1999 County and City Extra: Annual Metro, City and County Data Book*. Washington, DC: Berman Press.

Garofalo, J. 1987. "Reassessing the Lifestyle Model of Criminal Victimization." In *Positive Criminology*, ed. M. R. Gottfredson and T. Hirschi. Newbury Park, CA: Sage.

Garofalo, J., L. Siegel, and J. Laub. 1987. "School-Related Victimization among Adolescents: An Analysis of National Crime Survey (NCS) Narratives." *Journal of Quantitative Criminology* 3(4):321–38.

Goldstein, H. 1979. "Improving Policing: A Problem-Oriented Approach." *Crime and Delinquency* (April):234–58.

——. 1990. *Problem-Oriented Policing*. New York: McGraw Hill.

Gottfredson, D. C. 2001. *Schools and Delinquency*. Cambridge: Cambridge University Press.

Gottfredson, D. C., D. B. Wilson, and S. S. Najaka. 2002. "The Schools." In *Crime: Public Polices for Crime Control*, 2nd edition, ed. J. Q. Wilson and J. Petersilia. San Francisco: ICS Press.

Gottfredson, G. D., and D. Gottfredson. 1985. *Victimization in Schools*. New York: Plenum Press.

Gottfredson, M. R. 1981. "On the Etiology of Criminal Victimization." *Journal of Criminal Law and Criminology* 72:714–26.

——. 1984. *Victims of Crime: The Dimensions of Risk*. Home Office Research Study No. 81. London: Her Majesty's Stationery Office.

Gouvis, C., C. Johnson, C. Destefano, A. Solomon, and M. Waul. 2000. *Violence in the District of Columbia: Patterns From 1999*. Report to the D.C. Criminal Justice Coordinating Council, Washington, DC: The Urban Institute.

Gouvis, C., C. Johnson, and J. A. Roth. 1997. *Patterns of Violent Crime Committed Against Juveniles in the District of Columbia*. Final Report to the Institute of Law and Justice. Washington, DC: The Urban Institute.

Greenberg, S. W., and W. M. Rohe. 1984. "Neighborhood Design and Crime." *The Journal of the American Planning Association* (December):48–61.

——. 1986. "Informal Social Control." In *Urban Neighborhoods: Research and Policy*, ed. R. B. Taylor. New York: Praeger.

Greenberg, S. W., W. M. Rohe, and J. R. Williams. 1982. "Safety in Urban Neighborhoods: A Comparison of Physical Characteristics and Informal Territorial Control in High and Low Crime Neighborhoods." *Population and Environment* 5(3): 141–65.

Greenwood, P. W., K. E. Model, C. P. Rydell, and J. Chiesa. 1996. *Diverting Children from a Life of Crime: Measuring Costs and Benefits*. Santa Monica, CA: RAND.

Groff, E. R., and N. G. La Vigne. 2001." Mapping an Opportunity Surface of Residential Burglary." *Journal of Research in Crime and Delinquency* 38:257–78.

Harries, K. D. 1981. "Alternative Denominators in Conventional Crime Rates." In *Environmental Criminology*, ed. P. J. Brantingham and P. L. Brantingham, 147–65. Beverly Hills, CA: Sage.

Hausman, J. 1978. "Specification Test in Econometrics." *Econometrica* 46:1251–71.

Hawley, A. 1950. *Human Ecology: A Theory of Community Structure*. New York: Ronald.

Hayes, J. G., and D. B. Ludlow. 2000. "Gun Violence and Public Housing Environments." Paper presented at the Fourth Annual International Crime Mapping Research Conference, San Diego, California.

Hindelang, M. J., M. R. Gottfredson, and J. Garofalo. 1978. *Victims of Personal Crime: An Empirical Foundation for a Theory of Personal Victimization.* Cambridge, MA: Ballinger Publishing Company.

Hough, M. 1987. "Offender's Choice of Target: Findings from Victim Surveys." *Journal of Quantitative Criminology* 3(4): 275–81.

Hoyt, D. R., K. D. Ryan, and A. M. Cauce. 1999. "Personal Victimization in a High-Risk Environment: Homeless and Runaway Adolescents." *Journal of Research in Crime and Delinquency* 36:371–92.

Hunter, A. 1985. "Private, Parochial and Public Social Orders: The Problem of Crime and Incivility in Urban Communities." In *the Challenge of Social Control,* ed. G. Suttles and M. Zald. Norwood, NJ: Ablex.

Jacobs, J. 1961. *The Death and Life of Great American Cities.* New York: Random House.

Jeffrey, C. R. 1971. *Crime Prevention through Environmental Design.* Beverly Hills, CA: Sage.

Kelejian, H., and D. P. Robinson. 1992. "Spatial Autocorrelation: A New Computationally Simple Test with an Application to Per Capita County Police Expenditures." *Regional Science and Urban Economics* 22:317–31.

Kennedy, L. W., and D. R. Forde. 1990. "Routine Activities and Crime: An Analysis of Victimization in Canada." *Criminology* 28:137–52.

Kiefer, N. M., and M. Salmon. 1983. "Testing Normality in Econometric Models." *Economics Letters* 11:123–27.

Kim, J. O., and C. W. Mueller. 1978. *Factor Analysis: Statistical Methods and Practical Issues.* Beverly Hills, CA: Sage.

Kleinbaum, D. G., and L. L. Kupper. 1978. *Applied Regression Analysis and Other Multivariate Methods.* Boston, MA: Duxbury Press.

Kurtz, E., B. Koons, and R. B. Taylor. 1998. "Land Use, Physical Deterioration, Resident-based Control and Calls for Service on Urban Street Blocks." *Justice Quarterly* 15:121–49.

LaGrange, T. C. 1999. "The Impact of Neighborhoods, Schools, and Malls on the Spatial Distribution of Property Damage." *Journal of Research in Crime and Delinquency* 36(4):393–422.

Lander, B. 1954. *Towards an Understanding of Juvenile Delinquency.* New York: Columbia University Press.

Laycock, G., and C. Austin. 1992. "Crime Prevention in Parking Facilities." *Security Journal.* 3:154–60.

Liao, T. F. 1994. *Interpreting Probability Models: Logit, Probit and Other Generalized Linear Models.* Sage University Paper Series on Quantitative Applications in the Social Sciences, 07–101. Newbury Park, CA: Sage.

Logan, C. H. 1975. "Arrest Rates and Deterrence." *Social Science Quarterly* 56(1):376–89.

Long, J. S. 1997. *Regression Models for Categorical and Limited Dependent Variables. Advanced Quantitative Techniques in the Social Sciences, Volume 7.* Thousand, Oaks, CA: Sage Publications.

Lynch, J. P. 1987. "Routine Activity and Victimization at Work." *Journal of Quantitative Criminology* 3(4): 283–300.

Marvel, T. B., and C. E. Moody. 1996. "Specification Problems, Police Levels and Crime Rates." *Criminology* 34:609–46.

Maryland Department of Planning. 2000. "Demographic and Socio-Economic Outlook for Prince George's County." Maryland Department of Planning, Planning Data Services. www.op.state.md.us/MSDC/County/prinproj.htm (accessed April 21, 2001).

Massey, J. L., M. D. Krohn, and L. M. Bonati. 1989. "Property Crime and the Routine Activities of Individuals." *Journal of Research in Crime and Delinquency* 26:378–400.

Mawby, R. I. 1977. "Defensible Space: A Theoretical and Empirical Approach." *Urban Studies* 14:169–79.

Maxfield, M. G. 1987a. "Lifestyle and Routine Activity Theories of Crime: Empirical Studies of Victimization, Delinquency, and Offender Decision Making." *Journal of Quantitative Criminology* 3:275–82.

———. 1987b. "Household Composition, Routine Activity, and Victimization: A Comparative Analysis." *Journal of Quantitative Criminology* 3:301–20.

Mayhew, P., R. V. Clarke, A. Sturman, and J. M. Hough. 1976. *Crime as Opportunity.* London: HMSO.

McManus, R. 2001. "Juvenile and Young Adult Firearm Use in South Carolina." South Carolina Department of Public Safety. www.scdps.org/ojp/Final%20–%209697 .pdf (September 5, 2001).

Messner, S. F., and J. R. Blau. 1987. "Routine Leisure Activities and Rates of Crime: A Macro-Level Analysis." *Social Forces* 65:1035–52.

Messner, S., and K. Tardiff. 1985. "The Social Ecology of Urban Homicide: An Application of Routine Activities Approach." *Criminology* 23(2):241–67.

Miethe, T. D., M. Hughes, and D. McDowall. 1991. "Social Change and Crime Rates: An Evaluation of Alternative Theoretical Approaches." *Social Forces* 70:165–85.

Miethe, T. D., and D. McDowall. 1993. "Contextual Effects in Models of Criminal Victimization." *Social Forces* 71:741–59.

Miethe, T. D., and R. F. Meier. 1990. "Opportunity, Choice, and Criminal Victimization: A Test of a Theoretical Model." *Journal of Research in Crime and Delinquency* 27(3):243–66.

———. 1994. *Crime and Its Social Context: Toward an Integrated Theory of Offenders, Victims, and Situations.* Albany: State University of New York Press.

Miethe, T., M. Stafford, and J. Long. 1987. "Social Differentiation in Criminal Victimization: A Test of the Routine Activities/Lifestyle Theory." *American Sociological Review* 52:184–94.

Molumby, T. J. 1976. "Patterns of Crime in a University Housing Project." *American Behavioral Scientist* 20:247–59.

Morenoff, J., and R. J. Sampson. 1997. "Violent Crime and the Spatial Dynamics of Neighborhood Transition: Chicago, 1970–1990." *Social Forces* 76:31–64.

Morenoff, J. D., R. J. Sampson, and S. W. Raudenbush. 2001. "Neighborhood Inequality, Collective Efficacy, and the Spatial Dynamics of Urban Violence." *Criminology* 39:517–60.

Newman, O. 1972. *Defensible Space*. New York: Macmillan.

———. 1980. *Community of Interest*. New York: Anchor.

Newman, O., and K. Franck. 1982. "The Effects of Building Size on Personal Crime and Fear of Crime." *Population and Environment* 5:203–20.

Newmann, F. W. 1981. "Reducing Student Alienation in High Schools: Implications of Theory." *Harvard Educational Review* 51(4):546–64.

Olweus, D. 1993. *Bullying at School.* Oxford: Blackwell.

Pablant, P., and J. C. Baxter. 1975. "Environmental Correlates of School Vandalism." *Journal of American Institute of Planners*, 270–77.

Park, R. 1926. "The Urban Community as a Spatial and a Moral Order." In *The Urban Community*, ed. E. Burgess, 3–18. Chicago: University of Chicago Press.

Perkins, D. D., P. Florin, R. C. Rich, A. Wandersman, and D. M. Chavis. 1990. "Participation and the Social and Physical Environment of Residential Blocks: Crime and Community Context." *American Journal of Community Psychology* 18(1):83–115.

Perkins, D. D., J. W. Meeks, and R. B. Taylor. 1992. "The Physical Environment of Street Block and Residential Perceptions of Crime and Disorder: Implications for Theory and Measurement." *Journal of Environmental Psychology* 12:21–34.

Pierce, G., S. Spaar, and L. Briggs. 1986. *The Character of Police Work: Strategic and Tactical Implications*. Boston: Northeastern University Press.

Popkin, S. J., L. M. Olson, A. J. Lurigio, V. E. Gwiasda, and R. G. Carter. 1995. "Sweeping Out Drugs and Crime: Residents' Views of the Chicago Housing Authority's Public Housing Drug Elimination Program." *Crime and Delinquency* 41:73–99.

Poyner, B. 1991. "Situational Crime Prevention in Two Parking Facilities." *Security Journal* 2:96–101.

———. 1994. "Lessons From Lisson Green: An Evaluation of Walkway Demolition on a British Housing Estate. In *Crime Prevention Studies. Volume 3*, ed. R. V. Clarke. Monsey, NY: Criminal Justice Press.

Raudenbush, S., and R. J. Sampson. 1999. "Econometrics: Toward a Science of Assessing Ecological Settings, with Application to the Systematic Social Observation of Neighborhoods." *Sociological Methodology* 29:1–41.

Repetto, T. A. 1974. *Residential Crime*. Cambridge, MA: Ballinger.

Richters, J. E. 1993. "Community Violence and Children's Development: Toward a Research Agenda for the 1990s." *Psychiatry* 56:3–6.

Roncek, D. W. 1987. "The Implications of Different Measures of Crime Rates: The Intra-City Case." Paper presented at the 1987 annual meeting of the Southwestern Sociological Association, Dallas.

———. 2000. "Schools and Crime." In *Analyzing Crime Patterns: Frontiers of Practice*, ed. V. Goldsmith, P. G. Mcguire, J. H. Mollenkopf, and T. A. Ross. Thousand Oaks, CA: Sage Publications.

Roncek, D. W., and R. Bell. 1981. "Bars, Blocks and Crimes." *Journal of Environmental Systems* 11(1):35–47.

Roncek, D. W., and D. Faggiani. 1985. "High Schools and Crime: A Replication." *Sociological Quarterly* 26(4):491–505.

Roncek D. W., and A. Lobosco. 1983. "The Effect of High Schools on Crime in Their Neighborhood." *Social Science Quarterly* 64:598–613.

Roncek, D. W., and P. A. Maier. 1991. "Bars, Blocks, and Crimes Revisited: Linking the Theory of Routine t the Empiricism of 'Hot Spots.'" *Criminology* 29(4): 725–53.

Roncek, D. W., and M. A. Pravatiner. 1989. "Additional Evidence that Taverns Enhance Nearby Crime." *Social Service Review* 73(4):185–88.

Rummel, R. J. 1970. *Applied Factor Analysis.* Evanston, IL: Northwestern University Press.

Sampson, R. J. 1985. "Neighborhood and Crime: The Structural Determinates of Personal Victimization." *Journal of Research in Crime and Delinquency* 22:7–40.

———. 1986. "Crime in Cities: The Effects of Formal and Informal Social Control." In *Communities and Crime,* ed. A. J. Reiss and M. Tonry, 271–311. Chicago: University of Chicago Press.

Sampson, R. J., and J. Cohen. 1988. "Deterrent Effects of Police on Crime: A Replication and Theoretical Extension." *Law and Society Review* 22:163–89.

Sampson, R. J., and J. Wooldrege. 1987. "Linking the Micro- and Macro-Level Dimensions of Lifestyle-Routine Activity and Opportunity Models of Predatory Victimization." *Journal of Quantitative Criminology* 3:371–93.

Sampson, R. J., J. D. Morenoff, and F. Earls. 1999. "Beyond Social Capital: Spatial Dynamics of Collective Efficacy for Children." *American Sociological Review* 64:633–60.

Sampson, R. J., and S. W. Raudenbush. 1999. "Systematic Social Observation of Public Spaces: A New Look at Disorder in Urban Neighborhoods." *American Journal of Sociology* 105:603–51.

Sampson, R. J., S. W. Raudenbush, and F. Earls. 1997. "Neighborhoods and Violent Crime: A Multi-Level Study of Collective Efficacy." *Science* 277:918–24.

Schmid, C. F. 1960. "Urban Crime Areas: Part I." *American Sociology Review* 25:527–42.

Schuerman, L. A., and S. Kobrin. 1986. "Community Careers in Crime." In *Communities and Crime,* ed. A. Reiss and M. Tonry, 67–100. Chicago: University of Chicago Press.

Shaw, C. R., and H. D. McKay. 1942. *Juvenile Delinquency in Urban Areas.* Chicago: University of Chicago Press.

Sherman, L. W. 1995. "Hotspots of Crime and Criminal Careers of Places." In *Crime and Place: Crime Prevention Studies. Volume 4,* ed. J. E. Eck and D. Weisburd. Monsey, NY: Willow Tree Press.

Sherman, L. W., P. R. Gartin, and M. E. Buerger. 1989. "Hot Spots of Predatory Crime: Routine Activities and the Criminology of Place." *Criminology* 27(1): 27–55.

Short, J. F. 1990. *Delinquency and Society.* Englewood Cliffs, NJ: Prentice Hall.

Sickmund, M., H. N. Snyder, and E. Poe-Yamagata. 1997. *Juvenile Offenders and Victims: 1997 Update on Violence*. Washington, DC: U.S. Department of Justice, Office of Juvenile Justice and Delinquency Prevention.

Simcha-Fagan, O., and J. E. Schwartz. 1986. "Neighborhood and Delinquency: An Assessment of Contextual Effects." *Criminology* 24:667–99.

Skogan, W. G., and M. G. Maxfield. 1981. *Coping with Crime*. London: Sage.

Smith, D., and G. R. Jarjoura. 1989. "Household Characteristics, Neighborhood Composition and Victimization Risk." *Social Forces* 68:621–40.

Smith, W. R., S. G. Frazee, and E. Davison. 2000. "Furthering the Integration of Routine Activity and Social Disorganization Theories: Small Units of Analysis and the Study of Street Robbery as a Diffusion Process." *Criminology* 38:489–521.

Snyder, H. N. 1999. *Juvenile Offenders and Victims: 1999 National Report*. Washington, DC: National Center for Juvenile Justice.

Snyder, H. N., and M. Sickmund. 1995. *Juvenile Offenders and Victims: A National Report*. Washington, DC: United States Department of Justice.

Somers, E. 1999. "School Violence and Kids from 2:00 to 8:00 p.m. Remains Key Priority." *US Mayor* 66(11):12.

Sparks, R. F. 1980. "Criminal Opportunities and Crime Rates." In *Indicators of Crime and Criminal Justice: Quantitative Studies*, ed. S. E. Fienberg and A. J. Reiss Jr. Washington, DC: U.S. Department of Justice, Bureau of Justice Statistics.

Spelman, W. 1995. "Criminal Careers in Public Places." In *Crime and Place, Volume 4*, ed. J. E. Eck and D. Weisburd, 53–66. Monsey, NY: Criminal Justice Press.

Taylor, R. B. 1980. "Conceptual Dimensions of Crowding Reconsidered." *Population and Environment* 3:298–308.

———. 1983. "Conjoining Environmental Psychology, Personality, and Social Psychology: Natural Marriage or Shotgun Wedding?" In *Environmental Psychology: Directions and Perspectives*, ed. N. R. Feimer and G. S. Geller. New York: Praeger.

———. 1987. "Toward an Environmental Psychology of Disorder: Delinquency, Crime, and Fear of Crime." In *The Handbook of Environmental Psychology*, ed. D. Stokols and I. Altman. New York: Wiley.

———. 1988. *Human Territorial Functioning: An Empirical Evolutionary Perspective on Individual and Small Group Territorial Cognitions, Behaviors, and Consequences*. New York: University of Cambridge Press.

———. 1997a. "Crime and Small-Scale Places: What We Know, What We Can Prevent, and What Else We Need to Know." In *Crime and Place: Plenary Papers of the 1997 Conference on Criminal Justice Research and Evaluation*. Washington, DC: Office of Justice Programs, National Institute of Justice.

———. 1997b. "Social Order and Disorder of Street Blocks and Neighborhoods: Ecology, Micro-Ecology and the Systemic Model of Social Organization." *Journal of Research in Crime and Delinquency* 34:113–55.

———. 1997c. "Crime, Grime, and Responses to Crime: Relative Impacts of Neighborhood Structure, Crime and Physical Deterioration on Residents and Business Personnel in the Twin Cities." In *Crime Prevention at a Cross Roads*, ed. S. P. Lab. Cincinnati, OH: Anderson.

———. 1998. "Crime in Small Places: What We Know, What We Can Do About It." In *Crime and Place: Plenary Papers of the 1997 Conference on Criminal Justice Research and Evaluation*. Washington, DC.

———. 2001. "Understanding the Connections Between Physical Environment, Crime, Fear, and Resident-Based Control." In *Crime: Public Policies and Crime Control*, ed. Wilson and Petersilia. Oakland: ICS Press.

Taylor, R. B., B. A. Koons, E. M. Kurtz, J. R. Greene, and D. D. Perkins. 1995. "Streetblocks with More Nonresidential Land Use Have More Physical Deterioration: Evidence from Baltimore and Philadelphia." *Urban Affairs Review* 31:120–36.

Taylor, R. B., and M. Hale. 1986. "Testing Alternative Models of Fear of Crime." *Journal of Criminal Law and Criminology* 77:151–89.

Taylor, R. B, S. A. Schumaker, and S. D. Gottfredson. 1985. "Neighborhood-Level Link Between Physical Features and Local Sentiments: Deterioration, Fear of Crime, and Confidence." *Journal of Architectural Planning and Research* 2:261–75.

Taylor, R. B., and S. D. Gottfredson. 1987. "Environmental Design, Crime and Prevention: An Examination of Community Dynamics." In *Communities and Crime*, ed. A. J. Reiss and M. Tonry, 387–416. Chicago: University of Chicago Press.

Taylor, R. B., S. D. Gottfredson, and S. N. Brower. 1980. "The Defensibility of Defensible Space: A Critical Review and a Synthetic Framework for Future Research." In *Understanding Crime*, ed. T. Hirschi and M. Gottfredson. Beverly Hills, CA: Sage.

———. 1984. "Block Crime and Fear: Defensible Space, Local Social Ties, and Territorial Functioning." *Journal of Research in Crime and Delinquency* 21:303–31.

Tedeschi, J. T., and R. B. Felson. 1994. *Violence, Aggression, and Coercive Actions*. Washington, DC: American Psychological Association.

Thrasher, F. M. 1927. *The Gang*. Chicago: University of Chicago Press.

Tobin, J. 1958. "Estimation in Relationships for Limited Dependent Variables." *Econometrica* 26:24–36.

Toby, J. 1983. "Violence in School." In *Crime and Justice: An Annual Review of Research, Volume 4*, ed. M. Tonry and N. Morris, 1–47. Chicago: University of Chicago Press.

U.S. Bureau of the Census. 2002. "Reference Resources for Understanding Census Bureau Geography." www.census.gov/geo/www/reference.html (accessed April 15, 2002).

U.S. Department of Education. 1997. "Fast Response Survey System: Principal/School Disciplinarian Survey on School Violence, FRSS 63." Washington, DC: U.S. Department of Education, National Center for Education Statistics.

U.S. Department of Justice. 1996. *National Crime Victimization Survey 1995–1996*. Washington, DC: U.S. Department of Justice, Bureau of Justice Statistics.

———. 1997. *Sourcebook of Criminal Justice Statistics 1996*. Washington, DC: U.S. Department of Justice.

Vélez, M. B. 2001. "The Role of Public Social Control in Urban Neighborhoods: A Multi-Level Analysis of Victimization Risk." *Criminology* 39:837–63.

Waller, I., and N. Okihiro. 1978. *Burglary: The Victim and the Public*. Toronto: University of Toronto Press.

Warner, D. and P. W. Roundtree. 1997. "Local Ties in a Community and Crime Model: Questioning the Systemic Nature of Informal Social Control." *Social Problems* 44:520–36.

Weeks, J. R., J. V. Kaiser, D. Chen, and M. T. Dolan. 2000. *Identification of Urban Areas at High Risk for Criminal Activity Through Image Analysis: What Are the Possibilities?* Report prepared for San Diego State University, Department of Geography and Commercial Remote Program Sensing Office, National Aeronautics and Space Administration. www.gis.usu.edu/docs/data/nasa_arc/nasa_arc99/reports/omegagro.pdf (accessed April 15, 2002).

Weisburd, D. 1997. "Reorienting Crime Prevention Research and Policy: From the Causes of Criminality to the Context of Crime." Washington, DC: National Institute of Justice Research Report.

Welsch, W. N. 2000. "The Effects of School Climate on School Disorder." *Annals of the American Academy of Political and Social Science* 567:88–107.

Welsh, W. N., R. Stokes, and J. Greene. 2000. "A Macro-Level Model of School Disorder." *Journal of Research in Crime and Delinquency* 37:243–83.

White, G. F. 1990. "Neighborhood Permeability and Burglary Rates." *Justice Quarterly* 7:57–68.

White, R. C. 1932. "The Relation of Felonies to Environmental Factors in Indianapolis." *Social Forces* 46:525–41.

Wicker, A. W. 1979. *Introduction to Ecological Pyschology*. Monterey, CA: Brooks/Cole.

———. 1987. "Behavior Settings Reconsidered: Temporal Stages, Resources, Internal Dynamics and Context." In *Handbook of Environmental Psychology*, ed. D. Stokols and I. Altman. New York: Wiley.

Wiebe, D. J., and J. W. Meeker. 1998. *Hourly Trends of Gang Crime Incidents, 1995–1998*. Irvine: University of California Press.

Wilson, J. Q., and B. Borland. 1978. "The Effect of the Police on Crime." *Law and Society Review* 12:3–26.

Index

behavior settings, 18
block face, 26
bus stops, schools and, 17, 36

census block, 26
Chicago School tradition, 3
collective efficacy, 8, 15–16
community. *See* neighborhood
contextual variables, 10–12
crime: generators (*see* generators of
  crime); measurement of, 28–30;
  opportunities for, 1–5, 8–11, 17–22;
  rates of crime, 28–30; and schools,
  2–3, 19–21, 47–49; social control
  and, 8, 15–16; violent, 17–18, 23–25,
  28–30
crime prevention through environmental
  design, 9
criminal victimization, youth and, 21,
  47–49

dangerousness of places, 1, 9–10, 21
defensible space theory, 1, 9–10, 14, 19;
  and guardianship, 36; and schools, 40;
  site features and, 9–10, 14; symbolic
  barriers and, 9; traffic patterns and, 9
disorderly milieu, 43–44
domain-specific models, 5, 47–49

ecological approach, 3–6; and family,
  11, 83; and housing, 9–10, 14,
  83–84; and neighborhood
  characteristics, 3–6, 8–15; routine
  activities approach, opportunities for
  criminal behavior, 4–5, 10–11; social
  disorganization and, 3–4, 7–8, 12–13
economic factors. *See* residential
  stability/instability; neighborhood
  structural processes
ethnic heterogeneity, 3, 17, 37. *See also*
  racial heterogeneity
exposure to crime, 8, 11, 13–14

family: female head of household, 16,
  25, 36–37; neighborhood
  characteristics and, 16; social
  disorganization and, 16
female head of household, 16, 25,
  36–37

generators of crime: bars and liquor
  stores, 2, 20; busy retail places, 13,
  35; public housing complexes, 2, 20;
  schools as, 1–3, 19–21, 23–25 (*see
  also* schools); transit stations, 2;
  youth hangouts, 13, 35, 47–48
geocoding, 28–29; intersections, 29

About the Author

Caterina Gouvis Roman is Senior Research Associate in the Justice Policy Center at the Urban Institute in Washington, D.C. Her research interests include the role of community organizations and institutions in crime prevention and neighborhood well-being; the development, maintenance, and effectiveness of community justice partnerships; and the spatial and temporal relationship between neighborhood characteristics and violence. She is currently partnering with a number of Washington, D.C., agencies to develop and examine strategies for reducing violence in D.C. neighborhoods. She is also directing several prisoner reentry research projects that examine issues related to housing and reentry. Her work on reentry has recently been published in the journals *Criminology and Public Policy* and *Justice Research and Policy*. She received a Ph.D. in sociology and justice, law, and society from American University.